KU-501-404

CREDO

The Catholic Faith
explained

CREED	SACRA - MENTS
MORALS	PRAYER

Fr. Marcus Holden M.A. (Oxon.), S.T.L.

Fr. Andrew Pinsent M.A. (Oxon.), D.Phil., S.T.B., Ph.L.

Catholic Truth Society

The main reference sources for CREDO are the Bible and the *Catechism of the Catholic Church*. All Scriptural citations are taken from the Revised Standard Version (RSV) Catholic Edition unless the following abbreviations are shown: NRSV, for a citation from the New Revised Standard Version; NJB for a citation from the New Jerusalem Bible. The abbreviation "ccc." followed by a number indicates a particular paragraph from the *Catechism*.

The publisher acknowledges permission to reproduce the following:- Pg 6: School of Athens, from the Stanza della Segnatura, 1510-11 (fresco), Raphael (Raffaello Sanzio of Urbino) (1483-1520)/Vatican Museums and Galleries, Vatican City, Italy, Giraudon/The Bridgeman Art Library. Pg 10: Expulsion from Paradise (oil on panel), Giovanni di Paolo di Grazia, (1403- 83)/Metropolitan Museum of Art, New York, USA, Giraudon/The Bridgeman Art Library. Pg 14: The Fall of Man, 1510 (fresco) (post restoration), Buonarroti, Michelangelo (1475-1564)/Vatican Museums and Galleries, Vatican City, Italy, /The Bridgeman Art Library. Pg 18: Our Lady of China, courtesy of Aid to the Church in Need. Pg 22: Christ Enters Jerusalem (vellum) by Ethiopian School, (18th century) © The Trustees of the Chester Beatty Library, Dublin/The Bridgeman Art Library. Pg 26: The Crucifixion (fresco), Giotto di Bondone (c.1266-1337)/San Francesco, Lower Church, Assisi, Italy, Alinari/The Bridgeman Art Library. Pg 30: The Holy Trinity, 1420s (tempera on panel) by Andrei Rublev (c.1370-1430) Tretyakov Gallery, Moscow, Russia/Bridgeman. Pg 34: Giving of the Keys to St. Peter, from the Sistine Chapel, 1481 (fresco), Perugino, Pietro (c.1445-1523)/Vatican Museums and Galleries, Vatican City, Italy,/The Bridgeman Art Library. Pg 42: Our Lady of Guadalupe, patroness of the Americas and protector of the unborn. Pg 46: Baptism of Christ 1450s (tempera on panel) by Piero della Francesca, (c.1415-92) National Gallery, London, UK/Bridgeman. Pg 50: Episodes from the Life of St. Augustine, 1463-65 (fresco), Gozzoli, Benozzo di Lese di Sandro (1420-97)/Sant' Agostino, San Gimignano, Italy,/The Bridgeman Art Library. Pg 54: The Last Supper or, The Communion of the Apostles, 1474 (oil on panel), Joos van Gent (Joos van Wassenhove) (fl.1460-75)/Galleria Nazionale delle Marche, Urbino, Italy, Alinari/The Bridgeman Art Library. Pg 58: Return of the Prodigal Son, c.1668-69 (oil on canvas), Rembrandt Harmensz. van Rijn (1606-69)/Hermitage, St. Petersburg, Russia,/The Bridgeman Art Library. Pg 62: The Marriage of the Virgin, c.1305 (fresco), Giotto di Bondone (c.1266-1337)/Scrovegni (Arena) Chapel, Padua, Italy, /The Bridgeman Art Library Pg 66: The Temptation of Christ by Duccio di Buoninsegna © the Frick Collection NY USA. Pg 70: Moses with the Tablets of the Law (oil on canvas) by Guido Reni (1575-1642) Galleria Borghese, Rome, Italy Lauros/Giraudon. Pg 74: St. Peter Baptising the Neophytes, c.1427 (fresco), Masaccio, Tommaso (1401-28)/Brancacci Chapel, Santa Maria del Carmine, Florence, Italy,/The Bridgeman Art Library. Pg 78: Tabletop of the Seven Deadly Sins and the Four Last Things (oil on panel), Bosch, Hieronymus (c.1450-1516)/Prado, Madrid, Spain, Giraudon/The Bridgeman Art Library. Pg 86: The Virgin in Prayer, 1640-50 (oil on canvas) by Il Sassoferrato (Giovanni Battista Salvi) (1609-85) National Gallery, London, UK/Bridgeman. Pg 90: Maesta: eleven scenes from the Passion, 1308-11 (tempera on panel), Duccio di Buoninsegna, (c.1278-1318)/Museo dell'Opera del Duomo, Siena, Italy, Alinari/The Bridgeman Art Library. Pg 94: The Adoration of the Mystic Lamb from the Ghent Altarpiece, detail of Angels Adoring the Mystic Lamb, 1432 (tempera on panel), Eyck, Hubert (c.1370-1426) & Jan van (1390-1441)/St. Bavo Cathedral, Ghent, Belgium,/The Bridgeman Art Library. Pg 98: The Light of the World, c.1851-53, Hunt, William Holman (1827-1910)/Keble College, Oxford, UK,/The Bridgeman Art Library. Pg 102: Richard II Presented to the Virgin and Child by his Patron Saint John the Baptist and Saints Edward and Edmund, c.1395-99 (egg on panel), Master of the Wilton Diptych, (fl.c.1395-99)/National Gallery, London, UK,/The Bridgeman Art Library. (For those images where identifying copyright has been unsuccessful, the publisher would be grateful for information to trace copyright ownership).

2

Contents

Introduction 5

Creed

The Meaning of Life...7
Creation and Fall...11
Salvation History...15
The Incarnation...19
The Life of Christ...23
The Paschal Mystery...27
The Trinity...31
The Church...35
Scripture and Tradition...39
Mary and the Four Last Things 43

Sacraments

Liturgy and Sacraments...47
Baptism and Confirmation...51
The Eucharist 55
Confession and Anointing...59
Marriage and Holy Orders...63

Morals

Moral Action..67
Natural Law and the Ten Commandments 71
Grace and the Beatitudes..75
Virtues and Vices 79
Christian Life in the World 83

Prayer

The Life of Prayer..87
The Lord's Prayer 91
Praying the Mass 95
The Practice of Confession 99
Catholic Devotions...103

Further Reading 107
Subject Index 109

**A Prayer of St Thomas Aquinas
who always prayed before study**

*Bestow upon me, O God, an understanding that knows
you, wisdom in finding you, a way of life that is pleasing
to you, perseverance that faithfully waits for you, and
confidence that I shall embrace you at the last. Amen.*

Introduction

The CREDO pocket guide presents a concise and attractive introduction to the faith and life of the Catholic Church. It is based on the *Catechism of the Catholic Church* and is structured in the same fourfold way: Creed, Sacraments, Morals and Prayer.

This guide is for anyone who wants a convenient and easy-to-use explanation of the Catholic Faith. As such, it can be an effective tool to assist evangelisation. In addition, it may help members of the Church who wish to deepen or refresh their own knowledge. It also serves as a summary of the essential truths of the faith for those involved in catechetical courses and the *Rite of Christian Initiation for Adults* (RCIA).

It is hoped that the inclusion of works of art will help convey a rich experience of the Catholic Faith, an experience that will contribute to achieving the true purpose of our lives: to prepare for heaven and the vision of God face to face.

> *Go, therefore, make disciples of all nations; baptise them in the name of the Father and of the Son and of the Holy Spirit, and teach them to observe all the commands I gave you. And behold, I am with you always; yes, to the end of time.*
>
> Mt 28:19-20

An expanded version of this pocket guide, in a complete multimedia course, is available from CTS in its *Evangelium* series.

Detail from *The School of Athens* by Raphael Sanzio
Plato and Aristotle were philosophers who discovered profound truths about
God, the soul, the world and the meaning of life.

The Meaning of Life

The meaning of life refers to the most fundamental reasons for the existence of the world and ourselves.

Why?

As a child grows up, the most persistent question he or she will tend to ask is 'why?' As human beings we not only ask what things are but also why they are. The philosopher Aristotle said that this desire is universal, *"All people by nature desire to know!"* .

The question 'why?' can also be applied to the whole universe and to human beings. Why is the universe here? Why are we here? What is the goal of human life? Men and women throughout history have attempted to answer these questions.

What is the 'first be-cause'?

All the things we see in the universe are caused by other things. Many thinkers have concluded that this chain of causes cannot go on forever. There must be a 'first be-cause', a necessary, eternal and unchanging 'first cause' which creates and sustains everything else that exists. This first cause is what people naturally call 'God'.

In addition, the universe shows evidence of many processes that are ordered towards things of great complexity and beauty. The complex order and evident goodness of such things encourages belief in a God who created them.

What is 'God'?

'God' is what people rationally recognize as the single, all powerful and unchanging cause and purpose of things. This knowledge can be attained through reason, but raises further questions about the life of God and our relationship with God.

For Aristotle, 'God' was the unmoved mover. For Plato, he was the unchanging good. For Anselm, he was *'that greater than which nothing can be conceived'*. For Newton, he was the architect of the laws of nature. Einstein often referred to the first cause of the intelligibility of the universe using the language of 'God' or the 'mind of God'.

Christian faith holds that the answers to the questions of God and his relationship to us have been revealed by Jesus Christ.

What are Human Beings?

Human beings differ from all other living beings on earth. Although we are animals, we also have the capacity *to know* and to communicate intelligently using *language*. This capacity to know is not just based on sensory perception and habit, but is an ability to know *what* and *why* a thing is. Without this capacity we would have no science or philosophy.

Human beings also have a unique ability *to choose*, which gives rise to an enormous variety of human work and action, both good and evil. Many philosophers have realised that the kind of being who *knows* and *chooses* in this way must have some quality that is different from material beings in general, which are subject to change and decay. They therefore infer that we have immortal souls that do not perish when our bodies die.

What is human happiness?

As human beings we want happiness – something complete, fulfilling, pleasurable and permanent. As well as the good things that all of us need, many great thinkers have realised that our happiness must also somehow involve *knowing* God.

You have made us for yourself and our hearts are restless till they rest in you.
St Augustine, *Confessions*, I.1.1 (ccc. 30; c.f. 1718)

Happiness, however, appears to elude us. In this life we experience many partial and temporary joys, but none of these truly bring fulfilment. Furthermore, there is much pain and suffering in life, and our bodies decay and die. Nevertheless, knowing there is a good God, human beings have never abandoned their abiding hope for lasting joy.

What does God offer us?

Christianity affirms God's goodness and desire for our happiness. However, at the heart of the Christian gospel is an offer of something that utterly surpasses all human desire – nothing less than a sharing in God's own divine life and blessedness. It is only by responding to this invitation of friendship with God that we also find our natural fulfilment. St Paul speaks of this great gift and promise as follows:

What no eye has seen, nor ear heard, nor the human heart conceived, what God has prepared for those who love him.   1 Co 2:9 NRSV

The pages of this pocket guide present the truth of God and his offer of happiness as revealed by Jesus Christ through his Church. This is the true meaning of life.

Detail from *The Expulsion from Paradise* by Giovanni di Paolo
God is shown as Creator of the universe. He is depicted as holding back his
cloak, showing that He is distinct from the cosmos of created things.

Creation and Fall

What is Creation?

Creation is the special act by which God freely creates all
things that exist out of nothing.

What do philosophy and science say?

Philosophy shows that the universe has a necessary cause, but
cannot tell us if the universe has always existed. According to
the 'Big Bang' theory (first proposed by a Catholic priest,
Monsignor Georges Lemaître), the universe developed from a
compact, primitive and fiery state. Science, however, cannot
investigate causes beyond the physical universe.

God, however, has revealed that the universe had a beginning
and was created 'out of nothing' – out of no other pre-existing
thing, *"In the beginning, God created the heavens and the earth"* (Gn 1:1).

What is special about human beings?

Scripture testifies that human beings are unique in having a
material body and a spiritual soul. Each soul is *directly* created
by God. Human beings are *persons*, not merely things or even
animals, and are therefore of the greatest worth and dignity.

The account in Genesis is not a scientific treatise, but is
God's way of revealing to us certain truths about creation

and our origins. It reveals that at some point in time God created one man and one woman with a material body and, uniquely among animals, a spiritual soul. In Genesis these parents of the human race are called Adam, meaning 'man', and Eve, *"the mother of all those who live"* (Gn 1:20). This teaching does not exclude the possible evolution of the human body from already existing and living matter.

God has revealed that he created Adam and Eve *without defect* and with special gifts: freedom from disordered desires; bodily immortality; freedom from suffering; extraordinary gifts of knowledge. Above all, God gave them grace, enabling them to enjoy his intimate friendship. This relationship was to culminate in the perfect and lasting vision of God.

All these gifts and graces *should* have been passed on to the whole human race, including ourselves.

What is the Fall?

The Fall is the historical event of the first parents of the human race freely choosing to disobey God and suffering serious consequences for themselves and all subsequent generations.

What was the event of the Fall?

Revelation confirms that at the root of the world's disorder is an *actual, personal* sin of mankind's first parents. The event of the Fall is revealed by God and presented in Genesis in a figurative way. Echoes of this reality can also be found in the Creation accounts of other ancient cultures which refer, not just to sin in general, but an actual, historical event.

Scripture teaches that this Fall of human beings followed the Fall of a certain number of purely spiritual beings called angels. The leader of the rebel angels (demons), the devil, is depicted as the serpent of the book of Genesis who tempted man to imitate his own disobedience. The choice given to human beings was to make one simple act of loyalty to God.

> *The Lord God commanded the man, saying, "You may freely eat of every tree of the garden; but of the tree of the knowledge of good and evil you shall not eat, for in the day that you eat of it you shall die."*   Gn 2:16-17

The serpent or devil tempted our first parents with a lie, however, and they disobeyed God by eating from the tree.

What were the effects of the Fall?

By their sin, Adam and Eve lost their special gifts and perfect state, their intimate friendship with God and the promise of future glory in heaven. As descendents of Adam we inherit: *Original Sin* – the guilt of his sin as father of our race; *evil concupiscence and disorder* – a life of suffering, ignorance and discontent ending in death; *a state without grace* – a life without union with God and with no promise of heaven.

Was there hope after the Fall?

Unlike the fallen angels, the human race would not be lost forever. God in his mercy promised a means of salvation from sin and death. In God's plan of salvation history, there would one day be a new Adam and a second Eve.

> *"And I will put enmity between you and the woman, and between your offspring and hers; he will crush your head, and you will strike his heel."*
>
> Gn 3:15

Detail of *The Flood* by Michelangelo

The story of Noah's Ark shows how, through salvation history, God saves his people from the destruction that is the consequence of sin.

Salvation History

What is Salvation History?

Salvation history is the progressive unfolding of God's plan to save the human race from sin and death after the Fall. This plan gives the true meaning to the entire history of the world.

How does salvation history unfold?

After the Fall, man lost his friendship with God and suffered from sin and death. Through a series of covenants, God gradually re-established a relationship with humanity and prepared the way for the coming of Jesus, the Messiah who would bring a full and final salvation to Israel and the world.

God's covenant with Noah

After the Fall of Adam and Eve, the human race became more wicked, but one man, Noah, had won God's favour. God told him to build an ark to preserve his family and some animals from a flood that was to punish the world. After the flood, God established a covenant with Noah, promising to preserve life until the end of time, giving us the opportunity to be saved.

God's promise to Noah was perfectly fulfilled in Christ who remains with us *"to the end of time"* (Mt 28:20 NJB). Noah's ark prefigures Christ's Church that carries the faithful to salvation.

God's covenant with Abraham

God called Abraham to leave his own country, promising him a land, to make him a nation and to bless the whole world through him. With faith in God, Abraham settled in the Promised Land and became the father of the Jewish people.

God's promise to Abraham was perfectly fulfilled in Christ. Through him, God has established a redeemed nation, *the Church*, given us an everlasting homeland, *heaven*, and blessed all peoples.

What was God's covenant through Moses?

Abraham's son Isaac was the father of Jacob, whose twelve sons became the fathers of the twelve tribes of Israel. Eleven of these sons followed Joseph their brother into Egypt during a famine. These Israelites remained and grew greatly in number. Centuries later the Egyptians saw them as a threat and enslaved them. God raised up Moses to free his people, teach them his law and return them to their Promised Land.

God's work through Moses was perfectly fulfilled by Jesus, who freed us from the slavery of sin and gave the new law of grace. He founded his Church, the new Israel, on twelve apostles to bring us to our Promised Land of heaven.

What was God's covenant with David?

The Israelites conquered their Promised Land but broke the commandments, falling into sin and crises. They became jealous of the nations around them and demanded the judge Samuel to give them a king. After the unfaithfulness of Saul, their first king, God chose David as king. God promised David that one of his descendents would reign forever.

God's promise to David was perfectly fulfilled in Jesus, Son of David and King of the New Israel, whose reign will never end.

What did the prophets promise?

David's son Solomon built the Temple but broke the commandments. His successors divided his kingdom between north and south. In subsequent centuries the northern kingdom was destroyed. Finally, in 597 BC, Jerusalem and the southern kingdom were captured by the Babylonians who deported many of its people. Throughout this period, God sent prophets such as Elijah, Isaiah, Jeremiah and Ezekiel. These prophets called the people to repentance, social justice and peace. They also prophesised a future salvation, a new and everlasting covenant, a *Messiah* or *Christ*, '*the anointed one*', and a 'suffering servant', who would bear the sins of many.

God's promise of salvation, made through his prophets, was perfectly fulfilled in the Kingdom proclaimed by Jesus.

Who did John the Baptist herald?

Although the Jewish people returned from Babylon, there was no new king. They remained at the mercy of the Persians, the Greeks and eventually the Romans. Finally, a last prophet appeared, John the Baptist, calling the people to repentance and to prepare for the imminent coming of the Messiah.

"Prepare the way of the Lord, make his paths straight!"   Mt 3:3

Our Lady of China

Mary holds the new born baby Jesus -
God himself who has become man for our salvation.

The Incarnation

What is the Incarnation?

By the word 'Incarnation' we mean that God the Son took to himself a human nature for the sake of our salvation.

The word 'Incarnation' expresses the fact that Jesus Christ is not merely a man, a perfect man or even a saint, but God himself become man to save us and bring us back to God.

How did Jesus Christ come to be born?

The Annunciation is the historical event when God the Father, through the angel Gabriel, asked the Virgin Mary to become the mother of his Son. Mary, who was and always remained a virgin, questioned how she could conceive a child. The angel answered that this child would be conceived by a miracle:

> *"The Holy Spirit will come upon you, and the power of the Most High will overshadow you; therefore the child to be born will be called holy, the Son of God."*
> Lk 1:35

Mary gave her free consent to become the Mother of God, opening the way to our salvation:

> *And Mary said, "Behold, I am the handmaid of the Lord; let it be to me according to your word."*
> Lk 1:38

At the time of a census called by the Emperor Augustus, Jesus was born in Bethlehem, the City of David. We celebrate this birth at Christmas, meaning 'the Mass of Christ'.

The time came for her to be delivered. And she gave birth to her first-born son and wrapped him in swaddling cloths, and laid him in a manger. Lk 2:4-7

What are the titles of Jesus Christ?

Jesus	This Hebrew name means 'God saves', expressing well the purpose of the Incarnation.
Christ	From the Greek *christos*, meaning 'anointed one', a title of a priest, prophet or king. This word was also used for the promised *Messiah*.
Lord	From the Greek *kyrios*, often used for addressing God in the Bible.
Son of God	A title of the Messiah that also indicates the divinity of Jesus Christ.
Son of Man	A title of the Messiah that also indicates the humanity of Jesus Christ.
Son of David	This identifies Jesus as the promised heir of King David who will reign over the Church, the new Israel, for ever.

True God and True Man

The divinity and humanity of Jesus Christ were revealed throughout his life. Elizabeth hailed Mary as 'mother of my Lord' and wise men came to worship him at his birth. John's Gospel states that the Word, who is God, 'became flesh'.

The Incarnation in the Creed

The Nicene Creed (325 AD) is an ancient summary of Christian belief. It defines the two natures of Christ.

JESUS IS TRUE GOD

I believe in one Lord Jesus Christ, the Only Begotten Son of God, born of the Father before all ages. God from God, Light from Light, true God from true God, begotten, not made, consubstantial with the Father; through him all things were made.

He was, is and always will be God with the Father and the Holy Spirit.

He is *begotten, not made*, a divine person, not a created person like us. All created things came to be through him.

JESUS IS TRUE MAN

For us men and for our salvation he came down from heaven, and by the Holy Spirit was incarnate of the Virgin Mary, and became man.

He became man, body and soul, participating fully in human life, and remaining incarnate to unite humanity with God forever.

Mistakes about the Incarnation include: *Docetism*, which claims that Jesus only appears to be human; *Arianism*, which denies that Jesus is truly God; and *Nestorianism*, which claims that Jesus is two conjoined persons rather than one.

The Incarnation and the prayer *Hail Mary*

The *Hail Mary* is based on the Incarnation, combining the words of Gabriel and Elizabeth with the title 'Mother of God'.

Hail Mary, full of grace, the Lord is with thee. Blessed art thou among women, and blessed is the fruit of thy womb, Jesus. Holy Mary, Mother of God, pray for us sinners now and at the hour of our death. Amen.

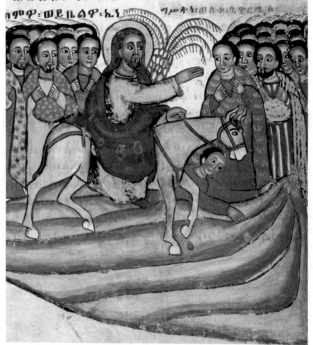

Detail of the *Triumphal Entry* from an 18th century Ethiopian manuscript

The dramatic entry of Jesus into Jerusalem fulfilled the Old Testament prophecy of the *Messiah* or *Christ* who would save his people.

The Life of Christ

What is the Life of Christ?

The life of Christ is the life that the incarnate Son of God lived upon earth from the time of his conception until his Ascension.

The principal events of the life of Christ

Conception and birth (c. 6 BC)
His miraculous conception in Nazareth and his birth in the poverty of a stable in Bethlehem

Hidden life (to c. 24 AD)
His thirty years living in Nazareth, known as the carpenter's son

Public ministry (to c. 27 AD)
His three year mission preaching the Kingdom of God, working signs and miracles and establishing his Church

Death, Resurrection, Ascension (c. 27 AD)
His submission to a cruel execution on a cross as a sacrifice for sin; his Resurrection and Ascension into glory

The common timescale of all human history is now measured by the coming of Christ. The words 'before Christ' (BC) refer to the years prior to his birth. The words 'anno Domini' (AD), 'in the year of the Lord', acknowledge his continuing reign.

The public ministry of Jesus Christ

JESUS REVEALED HIS IDENTITY

Jesus witnessed to his unique relationship with 'the Father' referring to himself as the only Son (Mt 21:33-41; Mt 11:27). He clearly asserted his own eternal existence and divinity by applying to himself the name of God revealed to Moses: *"Before Abraham was, I AM"* (Jn 8:58, c.f. Ex 3:14). He witnessed to his divine power by great nature miracles (Mt 8:26), and by forgiving sins, *"My son, your sins are forgiven"* (Mk 2:5).

JESUS EXPLAINED HIS MISSION

Jesus explained that he was to die for the salvation of the world (Jn 12:32) and to share with us the life of the Father, Son and Holy Spirit (Mt 28:19). His inaugurating of the Kingdom of God was shown by his victory over evil in forgiving sins, casting out demons and healing the sick (Mt 10:7-8).

JESUS TAUGHT HIS NEW DOCTRINE

Jesus taught through his parables and especially by the Sermon on the Mount. By word and example he showed that the greatest commandment of the law was love of God and neighbour (Mt 22:36-39). Just before his death he gave his disciples a new commandment to *"love one another as I have loved you"* (Jn 13:34), a love made possible only by sharing in his own divine love.

JESUS FOUNDED HIS CHURCH

In choosing twelve apostles Jesus established a visible Church, a new Israel (Mt 10:2). He gave authority to Peter and the other apostles to govern and to teach, *"Whatever you bind on earth will be bound in heaven"* (Mt 16:19). He also gave them new sacramental rites, *"Do this in remembrance of me"* (Lk 22:19). These superseded the ancient Jewish rites and empower us to be born again in Baptism and live the new life of grace.

Knowing Jesus Christ

We know Jesus Christ through reason and the gift of faith, which leads to personal friendship.

Knowing Jesus through reason

Through reasoned investigation we can know the life of Jesus, the world in which he lived and his teaching. The twenty-seven documents of the New Testament constitute the largest volume of written evidence in the ancient world about any one person. Non-Christian historians of that period also refer to Jesus Christ, in particular Josephus and Tacitus.

The New Testament documents were all written some twenty to seventy years after the public ministry of Jesus Christ. They were commonly accepted in the early Church as having been written under the authority of the apostles. The four gospels provide mutual corroboration of the events of Jesus' life. While they use a variety of styles, details and arrangements, a single clear personality emerges from the texts.

Knowing Jesus through faith

We also know Jesus through the supernatural gift of faith. This enables us to recognise Christ's divine personhood and trust in his saving mission. Our relationship with him is then cultivated through familiarity with his character in the Gospels, prayer, receiving him in the Eucharist and conforming our lives to the pattern of his life. This personal knowledge leads us to friendship with him as our living Lord.

The Crucifixion by Giotto di Bondone

The sacrificial suffering of Jesus Christ, his death and Resurrection heals us from sin and enables us to become children of God.

The Paschal Mystery

The Paschal mystery is the Passion, death and Resurrection of Jesus Christ by which he heals us from sin and enables us to become children of God.

The Passion of Jesus

The Passion refers to the sacrificial suffering and death of Jesus Christ by crucifixion on Mount Calvary. Jesus foretold these events and made it clear to his disciples that he would suffer freely for the salvation of the world (Mt 20:18-19).

After his Last Supper, Jesus was arrested in the Garden of Gethsemane outside the walls of Jerusalem. He was tried, found guilty and then handed over to Pontius Pilate who had him crucified. He was scourged, crowned with thorns and led to the hill of Calvary carrying his cross. He died between two thieves. As he died he said, "*It is accomplished*" (Jn 19:30).

What is the atonement?

The word 'atonement' describes how Christ's action saves us. The word implies both a repayment for our sins (*to atone*) and a reunion of God and humanity (making *at-one*). The atonement is accomplished through a sacrificial petition offered by Christ to God, the divine love of which utterly revokes the offence of all sins and bears the pain and cost of sin in itself. Only a person who was truly divine, human and innocent could make such an effective sacrifice on our behalf.

The atonement and ourselves

WHAT THE ATONEMENT DOES FOR US

Repays our debt of guilt	*"The Son of Man came ... to serve and to give his life as a ransom"* (Mt 20:28).
Gains mercy for us and repeals our punishment	*By his wounds we are healed* (Isa 53:5); *"This is my blood ... which is poured out for many for the forgiveness of sins"* (Mt 26:28).
Defeats the claims of the devil over us	*"Now shall the ruler of this world be cast out"* (Jn 12:31); *deliver those ... subject to lifelong bondage ...* (Heb 2:15).
Reconciles us to God	*In Christ God was reconciling the world to himself* (2 Co 5:19).
Fulfils Scripture and salvation history	*As a plan for the fullness of time, to unite all things in him, things in heaven and things on earth, making peace by the blood of his cross* (Col 1:20).

The atonement also teaches us the seriousness of sin by the bitterness of its remedy, and manifests the extent of God's love for us, *"God shows his love for us in that while we were yet sinners Christ died for us"* (Rm 5:8). By the atonement, Jesus has also given us the supreme example of sacrificial love, *"Greater love has no man than this, that a man lay down his life for his friends"* (Jn 15:13).

The descent to the dead

The soul of Jesus descended to the dead in the period between his death and Resurrection. Scripture refers to him *"preaching to the spirits in prison"* (1 Pet 3:18-20). In other words, Jesus released those just souls who had died before his coming and opened heaven to them.

The Resurrection of Jesus

What is the Resurrection?

The Resurrection is the bodily rising of Jesus Christ from the dead after three days in the tomb.

St Peter states that Jesus rose *physically*: "[we] *ate and drank with him after he rose from the dead*" (Ac 10:41), but his glorified body had extraordinary new abilities. He appeared at different times and places, and his body, though glorified and transformed in appearance, still bore the wounds of the crucifixion (Jn 20:28).

The physicality of the Resurrection of Jesus, witnessed by so many, rules out the claim that only Jesus' soul or ghost returned, or that only his message lived on, or that he merely revived, or that it was all an elaborate hoax.

The importance of the Resurrection for us

By his Resurrection, Jesus confirmed the validity of all he taught and did, showed that human life does not cease with death and manifested the reality of a glorified risen humanity.

What is the Ascension?

The Ascension is Jesus' physical departure from his disciples. This event took place after forty days of appearances and teaching following his Resurrection. Scripture records him *ascending* to heaven, which signifies the "*definitive entrance of Jesus' humanity into God's heavenly domain*" (ccc. 665). Jesus is now in heaven, where he intercedes and prepares a place for us, and from where he shall come again at the end of time.

The Trinity by Andrei Rublev

The similarity of the figures signifies that the three persons of the Trinity are equally God. The differences of the eyes, clothing and gestures signify the distinct relations of the three divine persons. The open table and chalice in the foreground invite us to share the divine life of the Trinity.

The Trinity

> The Trinity is the one God in three persons,
> Father, Son and Holy Spirit.

The Revelation of the Trinity

The revelation of the one God

The existence of the one God has been known to faith and reason throughout history. God chose to reveal himself as one Lord to the people of Israel, to teach them that he is the creator of all things and the single, true and exclusive object of worship. The Old Testament, however, gives glimpses of personal distinctions in the one God. An example is the use of the plural pronoun 'us' at the creation of human beings.

> *Then God said, "Let us make man in our image, after our likeness."*
>
> Gn 1:26

The revelation of the three persons

In the New Testament, when God the Son becomes man, he openly reveals the persons in God. First the relationship between the Father and the Son is revealed:

> *"No one has ever seen God; the only Son, who is in the bosom of the Father, he has made him known."*
>
> Jn 1:18

Jesus then reveals the relationship of the Father and the Son with the Holy Spirit:

> *"When the Paraclete comes, whom I shall send to you from the Father, the Spirit of truth who issues from the Father, he will be my witness."* Jn 15:26 NJB

All Christian life begins with Baptism in the singular name of the three divine persons, following Jesus' command:

> *"Make disciples of all nations; baptise them in the name of the Father and of the Son and of the Holy Spirit."* Mt 28:19-20 NJB

The three divine persons are the One Triune God or 'Trinity'.

The Trinity in Creed and worship

The Trinity is the source and centre of the Christian faith. The divine persons introduce each section of the Creed.

> *I believe in one God, the Father almighty.*
> *I believe in one Lord Jesus Christ, the Only Begotten Son of God.*
> *I believe in the Holy Spirit.*

What is the Trinity?

One substance, three persons

God alone reveals the doctrine of the Trinity. Human reason can know that there *is* a God; we cannot know God as he knows himself except from what God has revealed.

The fact that Jesus Christ reveals the relationship of Father, Son and Holy Spirit, tells us that these are distinct divine persons. Each divine person can properly say 'I', as when Jesus says *"I and the Father are One"* (Jn 10:30). Jesus also uses a masculine personal pronoun (translated 'he') of the Holy Spirit when he says, *"the Counsellor, the Holy Spirit, whom the Father will send in my name, he will teach you all things"* (Jn 14:26).

Nevertheless, the relations within the Trinity differ from those among human persons. Our relations are changeable, and established over time. By contrast, the relations of the divine persons are the very being or 'substance' of God. They are eternal and unchanging. This oneness of being, along with the distinction of divine persons, is expressed in the Trinitarian formula affirmed by the early Church:

The Trinity is one substance, three persons.

Mistaken beliefs about the Trinity

Modalism denies that the Father, Son and Spirit are three persons, and sees them as mere appearances, or masks, of one person. *Tri-theism* denies that there is one God, and claims that the Father, Son and Spirit are three gods. *Subordinationism* denies that the Son and the Spirit are equal in divinity to the Father, claiming that they are subordinate to him.

The Trinity and our friendship with God

God does not want us to relate to him merely as creatures to their Creator, but to enjoy intimate friendship with him by sharing the divine life of the Trinity. This is why all Christian belief is Trinitarian (for example, the Creed); all sacraments are Trinitarian (for example, Baptism in the name of the Trinity); all Christian life is directed towards union with the Trinity (for example, the virtue of charity) and all Christian prayer is Trinitarian (for example, the Sign of the Cross).

Christ handing the keys to St Peter by Pietro Perugino

The 'Keys of the Kingdom' symbolise the supreme authority of Peter and his successors, the Popes, in governing, teaching and sanctifying the Church.

The Church

What is the Church?

The Church is the mystical body of Christ, established by God on earth to gather humanity to divine life in heaven.

God desires all the faithful to be a single family, united to him and to one another in one 'mystical body'. This assembly is the Church, the body of Christ, which God has established as the *"instrument for the salvation of all"* (*Lumen Gentium* 9§2, ccc. 776).

The Church in the Creed

The Creed describes the Church as *"One, Holy, Catholic and Apostolic."* The Church is *One* because she has one founder, God. She is also one because her members are united in one faith, sharing the same sacraments under one head, Christ, and the Pope, his vicar on earth. The Church is *Holy* because she is founded by God, and because her members are the baptised. She is also called holy because it is through her ministry that sinners receive Christ's forgiveness and become holy. The Church is *Catholic*, which means 'universal', because she is for all races and nations in all ages. She is also called 'universal' because all salvation comes through her. The Church is *Apostolic* because her faith and practices have come to her from the apostles, and because her leaders, the bishops, are the successors of the apostles. She is also called apostolic because she is 'sent out' to preach the Gospel to all creation.

The foundation of the Church by Christ

Jesus Christ established a group of followers under twelve leaders he called 'Apostles', the first bishops of his Church. He gave one of them, Simon Peter, overall authority.

> *"You are Peter, and on this rock I will build my church, and the powers of death shall not prevail against it. I will give you the keys of the kingdom of heaven, and whatever you bind on earth shall be bound in heaven, and whatever you loose on earth shall be loosed in heaven."*
>
> Mt 16:18-19

Jesus gave his disciples his teaching to pass on to all peoples. This teaching, found in Scripture and Tradition, is interpreted by the Church with the authority of Christ (1 Tm 3:14-15).

Jesus also established the sacraments to supersede the rituals of the Old Law, enabling his saving power to be ministered through the Church: *"Do this in remembrance of me"* (Lk 22:19).

Mistakes about the Church include: *an invisible 'church'*, which is the denial that Jesus founded any visible institution; *a church without a Pope*, which is the denial of the true hierarchical structure of the Church with bishops united to, and under the authority of, the Pope, the successor of Peter.

Where is the Church?

The Church on earth

St Paul calls the Church the 'body of Christ' (Eph 1:22-23). As a *body*, she has an ordered structure and a visible unity. As *Christ's* body, she is both a divine and human reality (ccc. 771).

The principal visible elements of the Church's structure are the bishop of Rome (the Pope), all the bishops of the world in communion with him, their priests and deacons, those in religious and consecrated life and the lay faithful.

Baptism is the means of entry into the Catholic Church, but not all the baptised are fully united with her. There are many Christians who are not Catholic, such as Protestant and Orthodox Christians. The Catholic Church believes that her essential structures and teachings are divinely established but recognises all that is good and true in other Christian communions. She is committed to the prayer and work for Christian unity which is called *ecumenism*.

The Church in purgatory

Since those who have died and are in purgatory are also part of the Church, the Church is also found in purgatory. This is why we in the Church on earth offer prayers and sacrifices for the purification and reparation of the holy souls of the dead.

The Church in heaven

The goal of the Church is to be united with God in the glory of heaven. The Apostles' Creed calls the Church in glory 'the communion of saints'. Although most saints are unknown to us, the Church has recognised that certain men and women, from all ages and states of life, are definitely saints in heaven.

We in the Church on earth are united in prayer with the saints in heaven. By our prayers we therefore honour the saints and ask for their intercession in our earthly pilgrimage, that one day we may enjoy their company in the glory of heaven.

OLD TESTAMENT

46 books
before the birth of Jesus Christ
Mostly written in Hebrew, c. 1200 – c. 100 BC

PENTATEUCH	FORMER PROPHETS	LATER PROPHETS	WRITINGS
Genesis	Joshua	Isaiah	Psalms
Exodus	Judges	Jeremiah	Proverbs
Numbers	[Ruth]	Ezekiel	Chronicles
Leviticus	I, II Samuel	Daniel	Job
Deuteronomy	I, II Kings	*and others*	*and others*

From early Tradition, and with her infallible authority, the Catholic Church accepts among the inspired books of the Old Testament: Tobit, Judith, 1 and 2 Maccabees, the Wisdom of Solomon, Sirach (Ecclesiasticus), Baruch and some additional parts of Daniel and Esther (ccc. 120). Protestant traditions set aside these books from the Old Testament, calling them 'apocrypha'.

NEW TESTAMENT

27 books
after the death and resurrection of Jesus Christ
All written in Greek, c. 50 – c. 100 AD

GOSPELS	ACTS	PAULINE WORKS	CATHOLIC LETTERS	REVEL-ATION
Matthew	Acts of	Romans	James	Revelation
Mark	the	Galatians	I, II Peter	*or*
Luke	Apostles	Ephesians	I-III John	Apocalypse
John		Titus	Jude	
		and others		

Scripture and Tradition

Scripture and Tradition together constitute the single deposit of revealed truth given by God to the Church and infallibly taught by the Magisterium.

What is Scripture?

Scripture is the single collection of 73 books called the Bible. It is the entire content of God's inspired written truth, revealing himself and his saving plan. Scripture is divided into the *Old Testament*, written before the birth of Jesus Christ, and the *New Testament*, written after his death and Resurrection.

Given its importance for salvation, God, through the inspiration of the Holy Spirit, has guaranteed that the Bible records faithfully and without error, everything that he wanted written and no more (c.f. *Dei Verbum* 11).

What is Tradition?

Tradition is what is revealed by God and handed on by the apostles, including those things not explicitly recorded in Scripture. 'Tradition' comes from the Latin *tradere*, which means 'to hand on'. The disciples taught before they wrote, and this oral teaching remained authoritative alongside written Scripture.

So then, brethren, stand firm and hold to the traditions which you were taught by us, either by word of mouth or by letter. 2 Th 2:15

Tradition expresses that breadth of divine teaching which cannot be exhaustively communicated in any one written form, as the apostle John states:

> *There are also many other things which Jesus did; were every one of them to be written, I suppose that the world itself could not contain the books that would be written.*
>
> Jn 21:25

Some truths of Tradition have subsequently been given dogmatic definition by the 'Magisterium'. Examples are the number of sacraments and Mary's Assumption. The definition and correct interpretation of the books of Scripture is itself the fruit of the Tradition. Other manifestations of Tradition can be found in the liturgy, art and music of the Church.

What is the Magisterium?

The Magisterium is the teaching office of the Church exercised by the Pope, the successor of Peter, and the bishops in union with him. With the authority of Jesus Christ (Mt 16:19) and the guidance of the Holy Spirit (Jn 16:13), the Magisterium teaches infallibly the revealed truth which Scripture and Tradition communicate.

> *I would not believe in the Gospel, had not the authority of the Catholic Church already moved me.*
>
> St Augustine, *Contra Epistolam Manichaei* 5, 6 (ccc. 119)

The principal teachings of the Magisterium are the dogmatic decrees of the papacy, the Creeds and the other doctrines of the twenty-one Ecumenical Councils of the Church since the time of the apostles. The first Council was Nicaea I (325); the most recent were Vatican I (1870) and Vatican II (1962-65).

How do I read Scripture authentically?

Any Biblical text, such as **Mt 27:1-2**, can be found from the name of the book (in this case **Mt** - the Gospel of Matthew), the chapter (in this case **27**) and the verses (in this case **1** to **2**).

Jesus Brought Before Pilate

27 When morning came, all the chief priests and the elders of the people conferred together against Jesus in order to bring about his death. **2** They bound him, led him away, and handed him over to Pilate the governor.

Example chapter and verse numbers: Mt 27:2

Read as one – The Bible must be read as a unified work in which God has chosen to reveal himself. Although made up of diverse texts from different times and cultures, the Bible reveals a single story of God's providence and salvation. The Old Testament points towards its fulfilment in the New; the meaning of the New Testament is fully revealed by the Old.

Read within the Tradition – God has entrusted the whole of Scripture to the Church. It is only by the Church's authority that the Bible's 73 books are recognised as the unified word of God. Only the Church has the right and capability of authoritatively expounding Scripture.

Read in the literal sense – The literal sense is the primary and direct sense of Scripture which God intends to convey through human agency. It is the meaning the writer intends, the interpretation of which is aided by the study of history and context. A literal reading does not mean a *literalistic* reading of texts intended as metaphors or parables.

Read in the spiritual sense – God has ensured that the realities referred to in the Bible can also point to *other* realities. *Allegory* links something mentioned in Scripture, especially in the Old Testament, to Christ or the Church. The *Moral Sense* links the things of Scripture to the Christian life of grace. *Anagogy* links the realities of Scripture to those of heaven.

A picture of the original image of Our Lady of Guadalupe, patroness of the Americas and protector of the unborn. The image, which is believed to be of miraculous origin, contains clear references to Revelation (Apocalypse), the last book of the Bible: *"A great portent appeared in heaven, a woman clothed with the sun, with the moon under her feet, and on her head a crown of twelve stars."* (Rv 12:1)

Mary and the Four Last Things

CREED

Mary, the Mother of Jesus

Mary was conceived immaculate. As a virgin, she became Mother of God by bearing Jesus. She was without sin, assumed body and soul into heaven, and is the Mother of the Church.

Why is she called 'Mother of God'?

Mary is called 'Mother of God' because she became the mother of Jesus Christ, true God and true man (c.f. Lk 1:43).

Why is she called the 'Virgin Mary'?

Mary has this title because she was and remained a virgin before, during and after Jesus' birth. Mary's question to Gabriel, *"How can this be, since I am a virgin?"* (Lk 1:34), and the angel's response, *"The Holy Spirit will come upon you"* (Lk 1:34) indicate that Mary's commitment to virginity was upheld by the miraculous conception and birth of Jesus Christ.

What is the Immaculate Conception?

Mary was herself conceived immaculate and spared from Original Sin and its effects from her beginning, fitting her to be the pure Mother of Jesus Christ. Scripture refers to Mary as 'blessed among women' (Lk 1:42), and 'full of grace' (c.f. Lk 1:28).

What is her Assumption?

Mary was assumed body and soul into heaven at the end of her earthly life (c.f. Rv 12:1). It was fitting that one without sin who shared so closely in the saving death of Christ, should be the first to share his Resurrected life in heaven.

The importance of Mary for us

In Mary we see our human nature gloriously restored and raised to heaven. She is the 'Second Eve', the mother of the redeemed (c.f. Jn 19:27), who protects and intercedes for us. The most popular prayer for Mary's intercession is the *Hail Mary*.

The Four Last Things

The Four Last Things are the two *inevitable* and two *possible* realities that we face at the end of our earthly lives.

What is death?

Death is the cessation of our present earthly lives, the moment of separation of our souls and bodies. Once dead, we cease to choose between good and evil: death irrevocably fixes our state for eternity. Although death came to us because of sin, not God's will, God has removed its terror for us and made it the path to eternal life. We should therefore remain in God's friendship, live each day as if it were our last and ask God for the grace of a holy death.

What is judgment?

First, there is a particular and unchangeable judgment which follows immediately upon our deaths. Second, as the Creed affirms, there is a final and universal reckoning at the end of time when Christ *"will come again"*. At this Second Coming he will *"judge the living"*, those still alive, *"and the dead"* united physically with their resurrected bodies. As we are to be judged by God, we should ask for his mercy and help to put our lives in order, examine our consciences regularly and practise Confession.

Human beings die only once, after which comes judgment.

Heb 9:27 NJB

What is heaven?

Heaven is our eternal home where God gives us the vision of his face and shares his divine life with us. Scripture describes heaven as a city or kingdom where the saints enjoy the perfected creation and the reward they deserve. Those who die in God's grace either go straight to heaven or first enter *purgatory*, a place of purification for sins and for reparation. We can truly hope for heaven since it is God's desire for us. We should ask him to prepare us for heaven even if we face sufferings on the way. It is good to make the saints our companions through prayer and to pray for the holy souls in purgatory (c.f. 2 Mac 12:44).

What is hell?

Hell is the eternal loss of the vision of God, and the place of punishment of the damned. It is the choice of evil and lack of repentance that leads to damnation. After the Fall, hell would have been the just end of our race. However, God in his great love has offered us salvation through the blood of Jesus Christ. We should ask God to save us from the 'fires of hell' (c.f. Mt 18:9; Rv 20:14) as he himself desires (1 Tm 2:4). We also have a duty to warn others, just as Jesus warned us, of the reality of hell and the need to repent and follow him in our lives.

The Baptism of Christ by Piero della Francesca

Any perfect act of worship involves Jesus Christ as our high priest,
the divine person in whom humanity and divinity are united.

Liturgy and Sacraments

What is the Sacred Liturgy?

The sacred liturgy is the true worship of God, enacted by Jesus Christ and his body, the Church, through the power of the Holy Spirit. It is a shared 'public work' (*leitourgia*) with ceremonies, rites and formulas established by Scripture and Tradition.

Why does the Church have liturgy?

The Church has liturgy in obedience to the will of God, most clearly expressed by Christ's command, "*Do this in remembrance of me*" (Lk 22:19). As the true worship of God, the Church's liturgy follows the ceremonies, rites and formulas established by Scripture and Tradition where the will of God is revealed. Liturgy involves common prayers, visual signs, symbolic actions, sacred music and the proclamation of Scripture.

The liturgies of the Church

The principal liturgies of the Church are those of *the Eucharist and the other sacraments*. All of these are led by sacred ministers, usually priests, and consist of official prayers, Scripture and sacramental actions. The liturgies of the *Divine Office* contain the prayers that priests, religious and many lay people pray several times each day – these consist mainly of the psalms. Other liturgical rites include the *Rite of Christian Initiation for Adults* (RCIA) and *Benediction* for the worship of the Eucharist.

When is liturgy celebrated?

Liturgy follows set times and seasons. *Advent* is the four-week period when we prepare for the coming of Jesus at *Christmas* and for his final coming at the end of time. *Lent* is the forty-day period of prayer, fasting and almsgiving that follows the pattern of Jesus' own fast in the desert. *Holy Week* and *Easter* are when we celebrate his redemptive death and Resurrection. *Ordinary time* covers the rest of the Liturgical Year.

Sunday, the day of Jesus' Resurrection, is the holiest day of the week. To go to Mass on Sunday and certain other holy days is obligatory for all of the faithful capable of attending.

What are the Sacraments?

Sacraments are signs established by Christ that cause what they signify. They heal us from sin and plant, nourish or restore the life of grace in us.

Why are sacraments important?

The sacraments are important because they make the power of the Paschal mystery of Jesus present to us for the sake of salvation. By these seven channels of grace, God makes us his adopted children and increases his life of grace within us.

The Seven Sacraments touch all the stages and all the important moments of Christian life: they give birth and increase, healing and mission to the Christian's life of Faith. There is thus a certain resemblance between the stages of natural life and the stages of the spiritual life.

ccc. 1210

What are the sacraments and their effects?

SACRAMENT	THE LITURGICAL CELEBRATION	THE EFFECTS
Baptism	The minister pours water over the head of the candidate saying, "*I baptise you in the name of the Father, and of the Son, and of the Holy Spirit.*"	The forgiveness of sins, the new life of grace and membership of the Church.
Confirmation	The minister anoints a person's forehead with chrism saying, "*Be sealed with the gift of the Holy Spirit.*"	The sealing with the Holy Spirit for the mature Christian life.
Eucharist	The priest consecrates bread and wine saying, "*This is my body which will be given up for you ...; this is the chalice of my Blood ...*"	The Real Presence; Sacrifice of Calvary re-presented; spiritual food.
Confession	The penitent confesses sins with sorrow and repentance. The priest gives absolution, "*I absolve you from your sins ...*"	The forgiveness of sins and restoration of grace.
Anointing	The priest anoints the sick person's forehead and hands with oil, praying the prescribed words.	The forgiveness of sins, spiritual strength and healing.
Holy Orders	The bishop lays hands on the candidate's head and prays the prayer of consecration.	The ordination of a minister to act in the person of Christ.
Marriage	The spouses express their consent to one another following the prescribed canonical form, usually before a priest.	The union of the spouses as Christ is united to the Church.

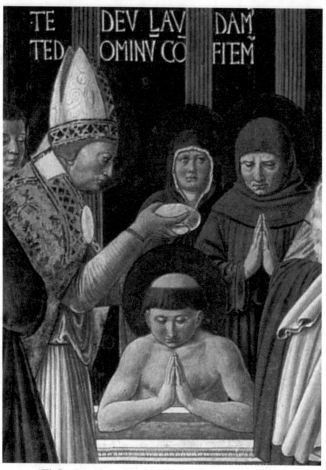

The Baptism of St Augustine by St Ambrose by Benito Gozzoli

The water of Baptism signifies the washing away of sin and
the new life of grace as an adopted child of God.

Baptism and Confirmation

What is Baptism?

Baptism is the sacrament by which we become Christians. It frees us from Original Sin, makes us children of God, temples of the Holy Spirit and members of the Church.

Why is Baptism important?

Baptism is of the greatest importance for us because it is the ordinary way of salvation for every human being (ccc. 1257). It is the gateway to the other sacraments and the whole Christian life:

"Go and make disciples of all nations, baptising them in the name of the Father and of the Son and of the Holy Spirit, and teaching them to obey everything I have commanded you."

Mt 28:19-20

What happens to us through Baptism?

The water of Baptism symbolises both washing and new life. The effects of Baptism are: *the washing away of all sins*, especially the state of Original Sin inherited from our first parents; *a new and supernatural life* as children of God and members of the Church.

"You were buried with him in baptism, in which you were also raised with him through faith in the working of God, who raised him from the dead."

Col 2:12

How do we prepare for Baptism?

An adult prepares for Baptism by becoming a *catechumen*, that is, someone who is being catechised (educated) in the Christian Faith. The formal process and rite for this is called the *Rite of Christian Initiation for Adults* (RCIA).

How does Baptism take place?

Anyone who believes and has not already been baptised can receive Baptism. Following early Church practice, the Church also baptises the infants of Christian parents, which sacrament bestows the initial grace of faith on those babies. Parents make a promise to bring up their child in the faith of the Church, until that child can make a personal act of commitment to Christ. New born babies should be baptised as soon as possible.

A sacred minister normally baptises. In cases of necessity, however, any person can baptise if intending to do what the Church does in Baptism. Baptism is conferred by immersion in water or by pouring water over the head, together with the proper form of words: "[*The person's name*] *I baptise you in the name of the Father, and of the Son, and of the Holy Spirit.*"

What is Confirmation?

Confirmation completes the Christian initiation begun in Baptism, making us spiritually adult by means of a permanent 'seal' upon our souls. In this sacrament the Holy Spirit also gives us seven gifts that enable us to see and act well spiritually. These gifts empower us to publicly proclaim the Gospel and to defend the faith against opposition.

Why is Confirmation important?

Confirmation is usually given by a bishop to those beginning to take on full Christian responsibilities. Confirmation is important because it equips us to live the Christian life in this world, helping us to attain salvation for ourselves and others.

Confirmation and Pentecost

Confirmation perpetuates in the Church the grace of Pentecost, when the disciples received the Holy Spirit to preach the gospel (ccc. 1288). Scripture describes his descent as like the 'rush of a violent wind' with 'divided tongues, as of fire' coming to rest on each disciple (Ac 2:1-4). They were filled with the Holy Spirit and began to preach in other languages.

What are the seven gifts of the Holy Spirit?

Three of the seven gifts of the Holy Spirit are for spiritual vision, that is, for grasping divine realities and created things in their proper order. These gifts are *wisdom*, *understanding* and *knowledge*.

The other four gifts are to assist good spiritual action. *Counsel* gives an understanding of what to do in particular situations. *Fortitude*, *piety* and *fear of the Lord* give perseverance, reverence for God and fear of offending God out of love of him.

How do we receive Confirmation?

Those about to receive Confirmation first renew their baptismal promises. Then the bishop prays over them for the coming of the Holy Spirit. Finally, the bishop anoints the forehead of each with holy oil (chrism), while praying the words, "*Be sealed with the gift of the Holy Spirit.*"

The Institution of the Eucharist by Joos van Wassenhover

Jesus feeds his disciples with Holy Communion, his own body and blood under the appearance of bread and wine.

The Eucharist

The Eucharist is a sacrifice, a presence and a food. As a *sacrifice* it makes present Jesus Christ's sacrifice on Calvary for our salvation. As a *presence*, it is Jesus Christ himself under the appearances of bread and wine. As a *food*, it is the nourishment of our souls by which we share in God's own life.

The Eucharist as Sacrifice

Uniquely among the sacraments, the Eucharist is also a *sacrifice*, the sacrifice of Christ himself. Sacrifices offer something up to God to honour him, to thank him, to gain communion with him and to make expiation for sin. The Eucharistic sacrifice of Christ achieves all of these perfectly.

Sacrifices in the Old Testament

Both unbloody and bloody kinds of sacrifice were prominent in the Old Testament. Sacrifices without blood included Melchizedech's offering of bread and wine and the yearly offering of the first-fruits of the harvest. The pre-eminent blood sacrifice was the sacrifice of Passover. Shedding the blood of the Paschal lamb and eating its flesh marked the 'passing over' from sin and death to freedom and life. All such sacrifices were commanded by God as provisional and prophetic, offsetting some of the effects of sin. However, these imperfect sacrifices of fallen humanity could never achieve our redemption or unite us to God (Heb 10:1).

55

The Eucharistic sacrifice of Christ

When Jesus began his mission, John the Baptist declared him to be *"the Lamb of God, who takes away the sin of the world"* (Jn 1:29). By these words John indicated that Jesus is the *perfect sacrifice* prefigured by the Old Testament sacrifices. Jesus confirmed that he would offer his flesh for the life of the world (Jn 6:51). At the feast of Passover, he took bread and wine and offered up his imminent death for our salvation.

> *"This is my body which will be given up for you ... for this is the chalice of my Blood, the Blood of the new and eternal covenant, which will be poured out for you and for many for the forgiveness of sins."*
>
> Words of Consecration in the Mass
> (c.f. Mt 26:26-28; Mk 14:22-24; Lk 22:17-22; 1 Co 11:23-25)

Jesus added, *"Do this in memory of me."* Therefore the Church, through her priests, continues to offer the same Eucharistic sacrifice. Christ's offering on Calvary and its salvific effects are thereby made present to all ages until the end of time.

> *For as often as you eat this bread and drink the cup, you proclaim the Lord's death until he comes.*
> 1 Co 11:26

The Eucharist as Presence

Is Jesus really present in the Eucharist?

Jesus promised to give food from heaven that would be his flesh and blood (Jn 6:51-56). He fulfilled this at the Last Supper, when he took the bread and said explicitly *"this is my body"* and when he took the wine and said *"this is the cup of my blood."*

This gift is also made present to us today. When the priest speaks the words of consecration in the Mass, the bread and wine truly become the body and blood of Jesus Christ. The Church calls this change 'transubstantiation' because the substance of bread and wine are really changed, becoming the substance of Jesus Christ himself. Jesus also said before his Ascension to the Father: "*I am with you always; yes, to the end of time*" (Mt 28:20). This promise is fulfilled in the real presence of the Eucharist in the tabernacle of every Catholic church.

The Eucharist as Food

Following Jesus' command "*Take this, all of you, and eat it ... Take this ...and drink from it*", the Eucharist has always been celebrated as a sacred meal. The benefits for us are:

Union. By consuming his life we become like him, and he dwells within us. For this reason the Eucharist is also called *Holy Communion*. As a meal, it also expresses intimacy with Christ and unity with the whole Church (1 Co 10:17).

Strength. By consuming divine food, we gain nourishment in the divine life that Christ has shared with us. The form of bread is a sign that the Eucharist gives us sustenance for our spiritual journey, and especially at the approach of death.

Promise. By receiving the risen Jesus, we also receive in the Eucharist the power of his Resurrection within us. As he promised, "*He who eats my flesh and drinks my blood has eternal life, and I will raise him up at the last day*" (Jn 6:56 and 6:40).

The Mass as a sacred banquet on earth is also our sharing in something far greater in heaven. Scripture refers to this gathering of the saints as a heavenly wedding feast, "*Blessed are those who are called to the Marriage Feast of the Lamb*" (Rv 19:9).

The Return of the Prodigal Son by Rembrandt

The moment of reconciliation between the father and son in the parable of
the prodigal son reminds us of the mercy of God in Confession.

Confession and Anointing

What is Confession?

Confession (or *Penance* or *Reconciliation*) is the sacrament by which we, repenting and confessing our sins, are absolved of sin through the ministry of a priest.

Why is Confession important?

Confession is important because it is the normal way we can be forgiven serious sin after Baptism. The regular practice of Confession is important because it helps us to deal with our sins quickly, develop a mature conscience and gives grace to resist temptation. The act of confessing itself bestows healing and a sense of release from the burden of sin.

How did Christ establish Confession?

Scripture states that only God can forgive sins (Mk 2:7). However, Jesus Christ gave his power to forgive sins to his apostles. The format of the sacrament has varied over time; however, the requirement for priestly absolution and verbal confession has remained constant. By these means, the mercy that Christ brought is perpetuated until the end of time.

"Receive the Holy Spirit. If you forgive the sins of any, they are forgiven; if you retain the sins of any, they are retained." Jn 20:22-23

THE ACTIONS OF THE PENITENT

Contrition: being sorry for my sins and having a firm intention to avoid them in future.

Verbal confession of sins: the telling of the kinds of sins I have committed and the number of times I have committed them. I must include all my mortal sins.

Will to make reparation: the intention to repair the damage caused by my sins and to fulfil the penance set by the priest.

THE ESSENTIAL WORDS OF THE PRIEST

After hearing my confession of sins, giving me a penance and hearing my act of contrition, the priest gives me absolution. The key words are, *"I absolve you from your sins in the name of the Father, and of the Son, and of the Holy Spirit. Amen"*.

Confession and Reconciliation

Sin damages our relationship with God and with the Church. Since it is the sacrament of Confession that reconciles us once again, this sacrament is also called 'Reconciliation'.

Repairing the damage of sin

The damage caused by sin needs to be repaired even after the guilt of the sin itself has been forgiven by absolution. For this reason the priest will give a penance during Confession. This penance is generally a prayer, a work of mercy, a sacrifice or an act of self-denial. By the mercy of God, these acts remove the punishment we deserve due to the effects of our sins. Indulgences offered by the Church are another means of remitting this punishment.

What is Anointing of the Sick?

Anointing of the Sick is that sacrament by which sick persons, through anointing with oil and the prayer of the priest, receive grace for the salvation of their souls and possible bodily healing.

Why is Anointing of the Sick important?

Anointing is important because it strengthens our souls and bodies at the approach of death, either to heal us or to help us to die in a state of grace. This strengthening is a crucial help because the condition of our souls at death completes our earthly pilgrimage and fixes our state for eternity.

How did Christ establish Anointing?

Scripture describes Jesus as the physician of our souls and bodies. He also promised that his disciples would lay hands on the sick, who would recover (Mk 16:17-18). The Letter of James (Jas 5:14-15) bears witness to the fact that the first priests of the Church anointed the sick.

What are the effects of Anointing?

The effects of Anointing are the *strengthening of the sick person*, the *remission of sins* (even when the person is incapable of confessing their sins) and possibly also *bodily healing*.

When is Anointing given?

Anointing is given when a person is seriously ill or in danger of death. Anointing should not be delayed until the point of death, however, and if the person subsequently recovers and relapses later, he or she can receive the sacrament again.

Marriage of the Virgin by Giotto di Bondone

This picture shows the marriage of Mary and Joseph. The dove represents the Holy Spirit, whose presence makes the consent of the spouses sacramental.

Marriage and Holy Orders

The Sacrament of Marriage

Marriage is that sacrament by which a baptised man and woman are bound together by vows to an exclusive lifelong commitment to one another and to accepting and raising children. In this sacrament God gives grace for the fulfilment of these duties.

What are the roots of Marriage?

God created human beings as male and female. This complementarity is the natural basis of Marriage, which throughout history has provided a stable, loving environment for the procreation and raising of children. Marriage is naturally monogamous and indissoluble but, due to the Fall, polygamy and divorce have often been tolerated. Jesus says this was not God's intention in creation:

> *"From the beginning of creation, 'God made them male and female.' For this reason a man shall leave his father and mother and be joined to his wife, and the two shall become one flesh. So they are no longer two but one flesh. What therefore God has joined together, let not man put asunder."* Mk 10:2-9

Christ and the sacrament of Marriage

The Catechism affirms that Marriage was *"raised by Christ the Lord to the dignity of a Sacrament"* (ccc. 1601).

The nuptial relationship of Christ with his Church is made present in sacramental Marriage, marking it with a specifically Christian character. St Paul confirms this by referring to Marriage as a *mystērion*, which can be translated as 'sacrament'.

> *For this reason a man shall leave his father and mother and be joined to his wife, and the two shall become one flesh. This mystery (mystērion) is a profound one, and I am saying that it refers to Christ and the church.*
>
> Ep 5:31-32

This link with Christ and the Church implies: *joy* in loving union and a foretaste of the 'Wedding Feast of the Lamb' (Rv 19:9); *sacrifice*, in that the spouses follow Christ in giving their lives for each other unto death; *fruitfulness*, in both the growth in holiness of the spouses and the acceptance of children.

What is necessary for the sacrament?

The spouses confer the sacrament on one another. They must vow freely, have no impediments (such as previous valid Marriages), be committed to one another for life and be open to children from God. Following the established rite, each must say, "*I take you ...*" in the presence of a minister and witnesses.

As Marriage is indissoluble until death, divorce is impossible. An *annulment* is the recognition by the Church that there was never a valid Marriage.

The Sacrament of Holy Orders

Holy Orders is the sacrament in which a baptised man receives the authority and ability to share in the particular mission that Christ entrusted to his apostles. There are three orders of this sacrament: episcopate, presbyterate and diaconate.

Where do Holy Orders come from?

Holy Orders come from Jesus Christ, who chose twelve men whom he called 'apostles'. He gave them the commission and power to *govern*, *teach* and *sanctify* (Mt 18:18; Mt 28:19-20; Lk 22:19).

How are Holy Orders passed on?

The apostles conferred Holy Orders on their successors, the bishops. These in turn ordained further bishops, priests and deacons through the laying on of hands and the prayer of consecration according to the rite of the Church.

The three sacramental orders

Bishops are the successors of the apostles and usually govern dioceses. They confer Holy Orders and normally administer Confirmation. United with the Pope, they exercise an infallible teaching authority in the Church. *Priests* are co-workers of the bishops, particularly in administering parishes where they also teach and sanctify the faithful through the sacraments. *Deacons* assist the work of the bishop and his priests. Following Christ's example, a promise of lifelong celibacy is the normal condition for receiving Holy Orders in the West, although a permanent deacon may be married.

The call to Holy Orders

Jesus taught us that the call to Holy Orders is his initiative rather than ours, "*You did not choose me, but I chose you*" (Jn 15:16). The call is discerned and freely accepted by the man who receives it. The Church tests this call and prepares the candidate for Holy Orders by means of spiritual, human, academic and pastoral formation, usually in a seminary.

The Temptation of Christ by Duccio di Buoninsegna

Christ was victorious over the devil's temptations in the wilderness.
If we call upon his help we can share in his victory over sin.

Moral Action

What is a Moral Action?

A moral action is any action that proceeds from our deliberate will. We have responsibility for such actions, all of which are either good or evil.

One of our unique abilities as human beings is to direct our own lives. This freedom enables us to be creative and to choose from among many possible good actions. Unfortunately, this freedom also enables us to choose things that are evil, that is, contrary to what is good for us and to what God commands.

God greatly desires us to choose only what is good for us. God does not, however, force us to do good. As long as we are alive here, we remain free to choose between good and evil actions. The effects of both kinds of choice are evident in human society.

What is sin?

A sin is a deliberate evil action: a thought, word, deed or omission contrary to God's will.

All sins are acts contrary to the will of God. They pervert some aspect of our human nature that he has created (such as greedy, slothful or lustful actions) or contravene some explicit command that he has given us (such as the prohibition against eating the fruit of the tree of knowledge (Gn 2:17)).

The root of all sin is *pride*, the attempt to make oneself into one's own 'god' independent of the order of nature and the obedience we owe to the true God.

Mortal and venial sin

Although all sin is evil, not all sin is equally evil. A sin is **mortal** if all the following conditions are present:

Grave matter	What we do, i.e. our chosen course of action, is gravely wrong.
Knowledge	We know full well, or should know, that this action is seriously evil.
Full consent	We freely consent to this action and could clearly have done otherwise.

Such sin is 'mortal' because it kills the divine life of the soul and deprives the sinner of heaven. The normal remedy for this sin is the sacrament of Confession.

All other sins are **venial**. They do not kill the divine life of the soul but they do damage and weaken us.

How can we do what is good?

One of the consequences of Original Sin is that it is not easy for us to do what is good. We tend to desire sinful things, a condition called *disordered concupiscence*.

A good *conscience*, formed through study of the moral law and good example, helps us to judge what is right. Establishing good habits in a well-ordered life and avoiding temptations also help. However, it is only with God's grace, through the sacraments and prayer, that we can achieve final victory over sin.

Moral Battle and Victory

What is the great battle?

The great battle is the struggle between good and evil which takes place daily in our lives. Our opponents are *the world*, *the flesh* and *the devil*. These conspire to intimidate us and tempt us away from following Jesus Christ. Our ultimate happiness depends on achieving victory over them.

The world, the flesh and the devil

The world is our enemy since it encourages evil and discourages good. By 'the world' in this sense we do not mean the Creation, which is good, but the collective evil influences of society that are opposed to God's will and our good actions.

The flesh is an enemy because of disordered concupiscence. Pleasures are good things created by God, but a disordered pursuit of pleasure in our fallen condition risks dominating our lives and enslaving us to sin. In addition, the fear of pain may prevent us from doing the good that we should do.

The devil and his fallen angels are our spiritual enemies because of their hatred of God and their desire to deprive us of eternal happiness. These creatures also have intellects that they use in a perverted way against us. As well as acting directly, they also use the world and the flesh against us.

The victory of Christ

Jesus Christ himself has conquered the world, the flesh and the devil. If we call on his help and make use of his gifts, we shall have all we need to fight and win the great battle (Jn 16:3).

Moses by Guido Reni

On two tablets of stone Moses brought Ten Commandments down from Mount Sinai, God's codification of the main principles of the natural law.

Natural Law and the Ten Commandments

MORALS

The Natural Law

The natural law, known by reason, is the universal moral law of human nature for living well.

The natural law is 'natural' because it is founded on what is good for human nature and because we can know it by our natural faculty of reason.

The natural law is valid for all people in all societies. Its principles can be understood by reason, even without faith. For example, dishonouring parents, murder, theft, adultery and lying are recognised by practically all human societies as being contrary to what is good for human life.

Christians have a duty to uphold the precepts of the natural law, both because these are rational and good in themselves and because they are part of God's will for us, 'written' into our shared human nature (Rm 2:14-15).

Natural and civil law

Civil laws apply the principles of natural law to determine what is good for particular societies. For example, the natural law forbids murder. Many more detailed civil laws are required, however, to extend this principle to defining, for instance, good medical practice and legitimate action in war.

71

Christians have a duty to promote good legislation and to obey the civil laws of the societies they live in (Rm 13:1 NJB).

Nevertheless, particular civil laws can sometimes violate natural law, examples being the racial laws of Nazi Germany or laws permitting the killing of the unborn. Legitimate civil laws can never oblige anyone to commit sin (c.f. ccc. 1903).

The Ten Commandments

The Ten Commandments are the ten universal laws given directly by God to Moses on Mount Sinai.

The Ten Commandments contain God's specific codification of the main principles of the natural law. God revealed these commandments (Ex 20:2-17; Dt 5:6-21) because Original Sin made it hard for human beings to discern good from evil (ccc. 2071). Jesus confirmed the necessity of the Ten Commandments:

Someone came to him and said, "Teacher, what good deed must I do to have eternal life?" And he said to him … "If you wish to enter into life, keep the commandments."
Mt 19:16-17

The natural law and the law of grace

As well as the Ten Commandments, Christians also follow the new 'law of grace'. The essence of the law of grace is to follow Jesus Christ in his Church, putting our possessions and lives at the service of God and others in charity. The law of grace guides us to heaven.

"If you wish to be perfect, go, sell your possessions, and give the money to the poor, and you will have treasure in heaven; then come, follow me." Mt 19:21 NRSV

THE TEN COMMANDMENTS (DECALOGUE)
Ex 20:2-17; Deut 5:6-21

1 **I am the Lord your God,
you shall not have strange gods before me**.
God, as our creator, wants us to love him above all else.

2 **You shall not take the name of the Lord your God in vain**.
God's name and all things dedicated to him should not be misused
or treated lightly.

3 **Remember to keep holy the Lord's day**.
God wants us to dedicate specific periods of time to him since
worship is of the greatest importance.

4 **Honour your father and your mother**.
The family is the basis of society. Respect and obedience is due to
parents and other lawful authorities.

5 **You shall not kill**.
To destroy or harm human life, made in God's image, is a
rejection of God's gift, the person and society.

6 **You shall not commit adultery**.
Marriage is the only legitimate context for sexual acts. Adultery
violates this sacred bond and destabilises families.

7 **You shall not steal**.
Personal property is needed for human well-being. Stealing is an
attack on personal and civic life.

8 **You shall not bear false witness against your neighbour**.
To lie or attack a person's reputation is an attack on human
dignity. It is an injustice in itself and leads to further wrongs.

9 **You shall not covet your neighbour's wife**.
To desire what is evil is itself evil. Impure thoughts corrupt our
minds and can lead to immoral actions.

10 **You shall not covet your neighbour's goods**.
God wants us to make full use of the gifts he has given us, not to
crave possession of the gifts of others instead.

The Baptism of the Neophytes by Masaccio

The shedding of garments for Baptism signifies repentance from sin. The running water signifies the washing away of sin and the new life of grace.

Grace and the Beatitudes

What is Grace?

Grace refers to those gifts that bring about a supernatural friendship with God. *Supernatural* means an elevation of human nature beyond what it is naturally capable of attaining.

Grace is a sharing in the life of God, as his adopted children, making us heirs to the kingdom of heaven. This life of grace far exceeds the mere forgiveness of our sins and our worldly improvement as human beings. In this new and supernatural life we become *partakers of the divine nature* (2 Pet 1:4), *co-heirs of Christ* (Rm 8:17) and *temples of the Holy Spirit* (1 Co 3:16).

Grace is first bestowed in this present life. It is fulfilled in the sharing of God's own happiness in the glory of heaven.

> *My dear friends, we are already God's children, but what we shall be in the future has not yet been revealed. We are well aware that when he appears we shall be like him, because we shall see him as he really is.*   1 Jn 3:2

There are two main kinds of grace. *Sanctifying* grace makes us children of God. *Actual* grace refers to the particular prompts and assistance that God gives us to help us act in ways leading to holiness. All grace comes to us from God by means of Jesus Christ (c.f. Jn 1:17) and his Church. The sacraments, in particular, plant, nourish or restore the life of grace in us.

The life of grace

Just as natural human life develops towards maturity, so too does the life of grace. As grace matures, building on our human nature, it also brings this nature to its own perfection.

LIFE OF NATURE	LIFE OF GRACE
Natural birth	Baptism (supernatural birth)
Philosophical virtues (for example, prudence)	Theological virtues (faith, hope, charity)
Food and drink	The Eucharist
Human society	The Church
Growth to adulthood	Growth in holiness
Human happiness	The vision of God

Mistakes regarding grace

Pelagianism is the belief that we can save ourselves. In this mistaken understanding, 'grace' is only the forgiveness of sins and the example of Christ. **Determinism** holds that 'grace' determines absolutely the eternal outcome of our lives and that our free wills have no significant role. **Modernism** holds that 'grace' is the same as nature. It claims that by nature we are one with God, or *part* of God or gradually *becoming* 'God'.

What are the Beatitudes?

The Beatitudes are eight states of blessedness proclaimed by Christ in the Sermon on the Mount (Mt 5:3-11). These states manifest the life of heaven on earth, bringing a foretaste and promise of joy even amid earthly suffering.

Blessed are the poor in spirit, for theirs is the Kingdom of Heaven.

Poverty of spirit enables us not only to use the goods of this world (such as riches and honours) in moderation, but to be willing to surrender all of them joyfully for the sake of the kingdom. (Mt 19:21)

Blessed are those who mourn, for they shall be comforted.

Mourning might not seem blessed because earthly joys are not themselves evil, although they can still come to dominate our lives. By grace, however, we set our hearts on heaven and are dissatisfied with anything less. (Jn 16:20)

Blessed are the meek, for they shall inherit the earth.

Meekness refuses even a proportionate and just response to evil. Jesus showed us the meaning of meekness when he submitted to being scourged, mocked and crucified without striking back. (Lk 6:29)

Blessed are those who hunger and thirst for righteousness, for they shall be satisfied.

Hunger and thirst for righteousness goes beyond doing our duties to our neighbour. It is an *eager desire*, like an appetite of hunger and thirst, to do works of mercy, so that those around us and ourselves grow in holiness. (Mt 6:31-33)

Blessed are the merciful, for they shall obtain mercy.

Mercy exceeds human benevolence and natural pardon for wrongdoing. It is a lavish bestowing of our time and goods on those who cannot repay us. It is also the gift of forgiving even outrageous wrongs against us. (Mt 5:43-44)

Blessed are the pure in heart, for they shall see God.

Purity of heart is far more than preserving oneself from the stain of sin. It is the gift of a God-like heart, to love God for his own sake with a single minded clarity and passion, and to love others as God loves them. (Jn 13:34-35)

Blessed are the peacemakers, for they shall be called sons of God.

Peacemaking goes beyond tranquil good order in earthly relations. It is the gift of establishing unity with others in a friendship founded on the desire for their supernatural good, that is, to reach our home with God in heaven. (Jn 14:27)

Blessed are those who are persecuted for righteousness' sake ... be glad, for your reward is great in heaven.

Persecution refers specifically to the trials that Christians face for preaching and living the Gospel. It blesses us in that it conforms us to Christ crucified, and holds the promise of great reward in heaven. (Jn 16:33)

The Seven Deadly Sins by Hieronymous Bosch

Clockwise from the bottom:
anger, envy, avarice, gluttony, sloth, lust and pride.

Jesus Christ is shown in the centre,
symbolising his grace to help us overcome these vices.

Virtues and Vices

What are Virtues?

Virtues are good habits, that is, they give us a disposition to perform good actions.

Human actions do not arise from a series of disconnected choices. We acquire dispositions that incline us to act in habitual ways. When these habits are good we call them virtues.

What are the principal virtues?

There are four main *natural* (*cardinal*) virtues that every good person needs. In addition, there are three *supernatural* virtues which are unique to the life of grace. The latter are also called *theological* virtues because they fit us for union with God.

NATURAL (CARDINAL) VIRTUES
Prudence – Deliberating well about what actions we should do
Justice – Rendering to each and to all what is due to them
Temperance – Curbing the passions that incite us to evil actions
Fortitude – Courage in adversity and constancy in difficult actions
SUPERNATURAL (THEOLOGICAL) VIRTUES
Faith – Trustful assent of the mind and heart to God's revealed truth
Hope – Expectant desire for attaining eternal life with God
Charity – An active will to seek the good of God and others and heavenly friendship with them

How do we achieve the virtues?

To some extent, anyone can acquire natural virtues through the discipline of repeated good actions and a well-ordered life. Nevertheless, we need the help of God's grace, by means of the sacraments and prayer, both to acquire the supernatural virtues and even to perfect and harmonize the natural virtues.

Above all these put on love which binds everything together in perfect harmony.

Col 3:14

What are Vices?

Vices are evil habits; that is, they give us a disposition to perform evil actions.

We sometimes develop vices which incline us to perform evil actions. These normally involve excess or deficiency in pursuing what is good. Often starting with small, venial sins, vices can quickly become ingrained and difficult to uproot.

The seven deadly vices

These seven vices are called 'deadly' because of their poisonous effects on the human soul, the difficulty that is often experienced in eradicating them, and the ease with which they lead to mortal sin. They are sometimes also called the *seven deadly sins* or the *capital sins*. Each of these vices has, as a remedy, a contrary virtue linked to the cardinal virtues.

The vices may promise an easier life but they ensnare and enslave us. By contrast, the virtues may seem difficult, but they lead to our true freedom and happiness as human beings.

The seven deadly vices and their remedies

PRIDE	HUMILITY
A denial of the superiority of the Creator and an inflation of our ego. It leads to excessive ambition, an over-estimation of our own strengths and the desire to be idolised by others.	A recognition that we are creatures and in need of God. It helps us to form a true opinion of ourselves, to disregard shallow popularity and to free us from self-obsession.
ENVY	**FRATERNAL CHARITY**
An anger or sadness that other people have gifts and possessions that we want for ourselves.	A gratitude for the gifts and talents of others and a desire that each and every person reaches their potential.
ANGER	**MEEKNESS**
A disordered state in which we take revenge on others, or an unfair opposition to a person or thing.	A self-control, not a weakness, which allows us to master our emotions when attacked or wronged.
SLOTH	**DILIGENCE**
A laziness or spiritual torpor that prevents us from doing what we can achieve and should do.	A readiness to always do what is needed. It makes even difficult tasks achievable.
AVARICE	**LIBERALITY**
An immoderate desire for possessions and gifts. Leads to injustice, stealing and indifference to the poor.	A generosity towards others in sharing God's gifts. It brings personal contentment with what we possess.
GLUTTONY	**TEMPERANCE**
A disordered love for food and drink. It leads us to eat and drink excessively and exclusively for pleasure.	A right use of food and drink for nourishment and pleasure. It leads to self-control in many other areas.
LUST	**CHASTITY**
A disordered craving for selfish and sensual pleasure (generally sexual). It leads to abuses of the body and the family and many addictions.	A proper use of our sexuality. It leads us to guard our heart and mind from evil influences, gives us freedom and allows us to love purely.

THE SIX PRECEPTS OF THE CHURCH
The obligatory minimum for the personal Christian life

1 You shall attend Mass on Sundays and holy days of obligation.

2 You shall receive the sacrament of Confession (Reconciliation) at least once a year.

3 You shall receive Holy Communion at least once during the Easter season.

4 You shall keep holy the holy days of obligation.

5 You shall fast and observe abstinence on the prescribed days.

6 You shall provide for the material needs of the Church according to your ability.

THE SEVEN CORPOREAL WORKS OF MERCY	THE SEVEN SPIRITUAL WORKS OF MERCY
Feed the hungry	Convert the sinner
Give drink to the thirsty	Instruct the ignorant
Clothe the naked	Counsel the doubtful
Harbour the homeless	Comfort the sorrowful
Visit the sick	Bear wrongs patiently
Visit the imprisoned	Forgive injustice
Bury the dead	Pray for the living and dead

"Truly, I say to you, as you did it to one of the least of these my brethren, you did it to me."

Mt 25:40

Christian Life in the World

MORALS

The Personal Christian Life

The personal Christian life is the confirming of one's life to the pattern of Jesus Christ.

Personal prayer life

Fidelity to daily prayer is essential to the effective living of the Christian life. The Church and her saints suggest certain common principles for Christians in every walk of life: **pray each day**, preferably at set times and especially at the beginning and end of the day; **learn some prayers** so that they can be recalled easily; **turn to God in prayer** even in daily work.

Personal knowledge

Knowledge is essential to the Christian life, because we cannot love what we do not know. It is helpful to: **set aside time for reading**, especially of Scripture; **discuss matters of faith** with others; attend courses and talks on the faith.

Personal sacramental life

Since the sacraments begin and sustain Christian life it is beneficial to make use of them more often than is obligatory. Daily Mass and monthly Confession are recommended.

Personal moral life

God calls us to follow his will even in our smallest actions and to offer daily sacrifices for ourselves and others. The lives of the saints teach us to: **ask God for grace** each day to grow in virtue and avoid vice; make an **examination of conscience** and moral resolutions at the end of each day; make **specific acts of charity and sacrifice**, such as fasting.

The Public Christian Life

The public Christian life is the conforming of one's own family and society to the pattern of Jesus Christ.

Christian society

We are called to pray and work for a Christian society that respects natural law, upholds the dignity of all people, is conducive to evangelisation and encourages everyone to follow their God-given vocations. The Church's social teaching encourages the common good through the principles of solidarity and subsidiarity. A special emphasis is put on charitable work to help the poor and those on the margins of society. We are all commanded by Christ to practice charity in our societies and especially the 'works of mercy' (page 82).

Evangelisation

We have a responsibility to proclaim the Gospel to others, a proclamation which is called *evangelisation*. We evangelise in a variety of ways, such as **praying** for conversions; **teaching the faith** to those around us; being ready to **give an account of the faith** to others when the opportunity arises.

Vocation

Every person is called to a particular kind of service. Marriage is the vocation of most people, although some are called to remain single. God also specifically calls some people to consecrate themselves in religious life or the priesthood. To discern and follow our vocation we need to: **pray** to discover God's will; **examine our talents** and the **contemporary needs** of the Church and the world; **pray for strength** to pursue our vocation when it has become clear.

Challenging the 'culture of death'

The attitudes and laws of many states have changed in ways that are contrary to respect for human life.

Abortion is the intentional killing of a child between conception and birth. It is wrong because it attacks the sanctity of a life made in the image of God. Modern contraceptive pills, which are partly and sometimes entirely based on synthetic progesterone, also sometimes act as abortifacients. **Euthanasia** is assisted suicide, which prevents God's completion of a life and corrodes respect for the old and infirm. It also prepares the way for the more general and involuntary killing of those judged unfit to live. **Human cloning** is the artificial duplication of human beings. In vitro fertilisation (IVF) is artificial non-sexual procreation. They attack the dignity of the child, the sanctity of natural procreation and lead in practice to the mass destruction of embryos. **Divorce, cohabitation and civil partnerships** destabilise and devalue the dignity of natural Marriage and the family as the true foundations of society. **Artificial contraception and homosexual activity** separate the gift of sexuality from procreation or married love altogether, contributing to a sexually irresponsible and sterile culture.

It is a work of mercy to avoid these practices ourselves and to help others avoid them by word and example.

The Virgin in Prayer by Sassoferrato

Mary's bowed head indicates her obedience to the will of God. Her beauty shows us that by prayer our souls begin to reflect the splendour of God.

The Life of Prayer

What is Prayer?

Prayer is speaking and listening to God and desiring to be
united with God and to do his will.

Why do we pray to God?

We pray because he *is* God. It is therefore right to adore him,
thank him and repent before him. We also pray because he
listens and will act on our behalf when we pray, and because we
come to know God, our greatest happiness, through prayer.

The principal activities of prayer

Christian prayer involves one or more of the following
actions before God: **adoration**, an act offered to God which
acknowledges his supreme perfection and goodness;
thanksgiving, an expression of gratitude to God for his
bounty in satisfying our spiritual and physical needs;
repentance, a recognition of the wrong we have done to
God by sin together with a desire to turn from evil and do
good; **petition and intercession**, the asking of proper gifts
or graces from God for oneself or on behalf of others.

Rejoice always, pray constantly, give thanks in all circumstances;
for this is the will of God in Christ Jesus for you.   1 Th 5:16 – 18

Mistaken ideas about prayer

Is prayer just in the mind? Prayer is not just in the mind. God acts when we pray and frequently causes miraculous changes in ourselves and in the world.

Does prayer seek a mental void? Prayer is not a mental exercise to empty the mind, as in Zen Buddhism or yoga. Prayer always has God and the things of God as its focus.

Is prayer just a technique? Prayer is never a ritual technique like magic, simply seeking power or other benefits. Christian prayer leads to the knowledge and love of God.

How Do We Pray?

VOCAL PRAYER

The mental activity of prayer joined to the physical one of words and gestures. Examples are the *Our Father*, the *Hail Mary*, the *Sign of the Cross* and grace before meals.

LITURGICAL PRAYER

The official and public prayer of the Church, such as the Mass or the Divine Office. It involves the Church as a whole rather than individual Christians alone.

MEDITATIVE PRAYER

Mental conversation with God often facilitated through Scripture, other holy writings and images that reveal him and his works.

CONTEMPLATIVE PRAYER

A simple and loving apprehension of God or divine things brought about by the Holy Spirit and the growth of his gifts in our souls.

Difficulties in prayer and their remedies

No time – Put aside time for prayer anyway. God will give our time back to us and will give success to all our good activities.

Boredom – Persevere, turn back to God and perhaps try another kind of prayer. Learn more about what prayer means.

Distraction – Avoid distracting situations, but do not be too anxious about failure: God knows and rewards our efforts.

Dryness – Do not make feelings the measure of success. God blesses those who pray even when they do not feel like it.

No answers – Persist and ask God to reveal his will. He may also want to give us something other than we have asked for.

What can help us to pray?

A regular time for prayer each day is a great help. It is also helpful to find a holy place, such as a church, or to set up a place of prayer in one's own home.

A Bible, Christian prayer books and devotional objects, such as holy pictures, a rosary and a crucifix, may also be used in prayer or may help to establish a holy place to pray.

Who can help us to pray?

The Holy Spirit helps us to pray as we ought (Rm 8:26). We can also ask the saints to aid us with their prayers. In particular, we can ask our most powerful intercessor, Mary, mother of all Christians, to pray for us and with us.

The Spirit helps us in our weakness; for we do not know how to pray as we ought, but the Spirit himself intercedes for us with sighs too deep for words.

Rm 8:26

Jesus Taking Leave of the Apostles by Duccio di Buoninsegna

Jesus teaching his apostles reminds us that the Lord's Prayer is the pattern of prayer that God himself has taught us.

The Lord's Prayer

What is the Lord's Prayer?

The 'Lord's Prayer', also called the *Our Father*, is the prayer Jesus taught his disciples when they asked him to teach them to pray.

The Lord's Prayer is the most perfect of prayers, because it was taught by Jesus Christ (Mt 6:6-13), the model and master of prayer. It is prayed in private, in groups and in the liturgy.

The structure of the Lord's Prayer

THE OPENING INVOCATION

Our Father, who art in heaven,

PETITIONS REGARDING GOD

Hallowed be thy name.

Thy kingdom come.

Thy will be done on earth, as it is in heaven.

PETITIONS FOR THE GOOD THINGS WE NEED

Give us this day our daily bread,

and forgive us our trespasses
as we forgive those who trespass against us,

and lead us not into temptation

but deliver us from evil. Amen.

91

The opening invocation

Our Father. We pray 'Father' because of our adoption as children of God through Baptism. We pray 'our', because this common adoption establishes a familial bond among all Christians. Jesus also promises that prayer in common is particularly powerful (Mt 18:19). To pray 'our Father' is also to acknowledge that, as his children, we should imitate him and avoid the things that make us unlike him (c.f. Mt 5:48).

Who art in heaven. This prayer acknowledges that there is a blessed place, the kingdom of heaven, prepared for us. There we shall see God face to face and dwell with him forever; *"the Lord God will be their light, and they shall reign for ever and ever"* (Rv 22:3). Praying these words also helps to raise our minds to heavenly things and increases our hope of glory.

What are the Petitions?

Petitions regarding God

Hallowed be thy name is not a prayer for something to be added to God, which is impossible, but for a greater personal knowledge and love of God in the world (Jn 17:6).

Thy kingdom come is a prayer that God's present reign on earth might increase and his everlasting kingdom be established by Christ's coming in glory.

Thy will be done on earth, as it is in heaven. This petition teaches us that our freely offered prayers help to accomplish what God wills for us. Uttering this petition also conforms our wills to his, *"not my will, but thine, be done"* (Lk 22:42).

Petitions for the good things we need

Give us this day our daily bread petitions God for our natural needs. The original Greek word for 'daily' also means 'super-substantial' (as it is translated in the Latin Vulgate version of Mt 6:11). Since this word indicates the Eucharist, this petition can also be understood as being for our supernatural needs. In both senses, this petition counteracts pride by reminding us of our dependency on God.

Forgive us our trespasses petitions God to forgive the debt of sin we owe him. Uniquely in the *Our Father*, however, the fulfilment of this petition is conditional upon a further action of our own, namely our willingness to forgive others. Jesus warns us explicitly, *"If you do not forgive others, neither will your Father forgive your trespasses"* (Mt 6:15). This petition also reminds us that we *ask* for, rather than demand, God's mercy.

Lead us not into temptation asks God to remove temptations or to give us the strength to resist them successfully. This petition also reminds us of our need to rely on God for victory against sin: *"This petition takes on all its dramatic meaning in relation to the last temptation of our earthly battle; it asks for final perseverance"* (ccc. 2849).

Deliver us from evil petitions God to set us free from all evil and especially from 'the evil one', the devil. It is also a prayer of hope since it reminds us of God's power and desire to save us, *"If God is for us, who is against us?"* (Rm 8:31).

Amen completes the Lord's Prayer. It means 'truly' or 'let it be so'. The word 'amen' also expresses the expectation that God will grant what we have asked.

The Mystic Lamb (Ghent Altarpiece) by Jan van Eyck

The saints in glory around the altar of the Lamb of God (Jesus Christ) remind us that the Mass on earth is our sharing in something far greater in heaven.

Praying the Mass

What is Praying the Mass?

Praying the Mass is the fully conscious and active participation in the Eucharist. This is the prayerful engagement in the Mass, aided by proper understanding, good preparation and the application of its power and blessings to our lives.

Preparation for Mass

We can prepare well for Mass in general by studying the structure and prayers of the Mass so that our participation is better informed. In addition, the more our lives conform to the Gospel, the better we shall appreciate the Mass.

We can prepare well for a particular Mass by going to Confession and by arriving in good time to pray before Mass. If receiving Communion, we must abstain for at least one hour beforehand from all food and drink except water and medicine.

During the Mass

We can participate well at Mass generally by being attentive and by uniting our own interior prayers to the words, actions and gestures of the priest. It is also important to: respond and sing clearly; listen carefully; try to understand what is happening; maintain prayerful silence; receive the Eucharist with the greatest reverence and genuflect with respect.

After the Mass

It is good to spend a few minutes of prayer in church after Mass. This is a way of thanking God for his blessings. It also enables us to be mindful of the resolutions we have made so that the power of the sacrament will be fruitful in our lives.

Difficulties with praying the Mass

Makes no sense. The Mass is rich in meaning and is unlikely to make immediate sense. Patience, prayer and study help us to appreciate its greatness.

Boredom. The Mass is a prayer and something we need for our souls. It is not mere entertainment. However, in practice it will engage us deeply if we attend to the words and think and pray about what they mean.

Inability to receive Communion. If conscious of grave sin, we should not receive the Communion without first going to sacramental Confession. To attend Mass devoutly has great value, however, even when we cannot receive Communion. We may still make a 'spiritual communion'.

The most important help in praying the Mass is to realise the supernatural and miraculous dimension of the Eucharistic sacrifice and the presence of heaven. At the Mass we join with the heavenly liturgy spoken of in the New Testament.

You have come to Mount Zion and to the city of the living God, the heavenly Jerusalem, and to innumerable angels in festal gathering, and to the assembly of the first-born who are enrolled in heaven, and to a judge who is God of all, and to the spirits of just men made perfect, and to Jesus, the mediator of a new covenant, and to the sprinkled blood that speaks more graciously than the blood of Abel.

Heb 12:22-24

The Structure of the Mass

INTRODUCTORY RITE

Mass begins with the Sign of the Cross, to commend the sacrifice to the Trinity. In the **Penitential Rite** all ask for forgiveness for their sins so that they may worthily share in the Eucharist. The *Gloria*, a hymn of praise and thanksgiving, is followed by the **opening prayer**.

LITURGY OF THE WORD

The **readings** from the Old and New Testaments, including the Psalm, are proclaimed. The priest or deacon reads the **gospel**, about the words and life of Christ. The **homily** explains some point of the readings or teaching of the faith. This is followed by the **creed**, a public prayer and profession of faith. Finally, the needs of the Church and the world are brought before God in the **intercessions**.

LITURGY OF THE EUCHARIST

At the **offertory**, the faithful offer bread and wine as a token of their own sacrifice to be offered by the priest. The **preface** gives thanks to the Father for his work of salvation and the *Sanctus* unites this to the heavenly worship of the angels and saints. At the *epiclesis* the priest extends his hands over the gifts and calls on the Holy Spirit to sanctify them and transform them. When the priest speaks the words of **consecration**, the bread and wine become the body and blood of Christ. He elevates the host and the precious blood for adoration. In the rest of the **Eucharistic prayer** the priest recalls the Paschal mystery made present in the Mass and intercedes for the living and the dead. Finally, he raises the host and the precious blood in a gesture of sacrifice and prays the **doxology**. The faithful assent with an '**Amen**'.

COMMUNION RITE

The faithful pray together the **Lord's Prayer** and express their unity and forgiveness in the **Sign of Peace**. While all pray the **Lamb of God**, the priest breaks the host. After the priest raises the host, all acknowledge their unworthiness and God's healing mercy. The priest then receives **Holy Communion** and distributes it to the people.

CONCLUDING RITE

The priest **blesses** and sends the faithful out on mission.

The Light of the World by Holman Hunt

Jesus Christ knocks at the door of our souls. Confession opens the door, allowing him to bring the light of his grace into our souls.

The Practice of Confession

The practice of Confession is the means by which we receive absolution of our sins; the sacrament also helps us to avoid sin and grow in virtue.

When should we go to Confession?

We should go to Confession at least once a year, most fittingly in preparation for Easter. More regular Confession, such as once a month, is a great help towards spiritual growth. We should also go to Confession when aware of serious sin.

How should we prepare for Confession?

We should prepare by an examination of conscience, being sorry for our sins, resolving not to commit them again and being ready to do penance. It is important to pray before Confession and to ask the help of Mary and the saints.

What should we be ready to confess?

We should be ready to confess all mortal sins and it is good, though not strictly necessary, to confess any venial sins. For each kind of sin we need to confess the number of times, as well as we can remember (for example, "*I lied three times*" or "*several times*" or "*many times*"). The only other details we need to add are those that change the seriousness of the sin (for example, "*I lied to hurt someone*" or "*I lied to try to help someone*").

Difficulties about Confession

Fear. Both God and the priest welcome us with joy. The priest is bound by a seal of absolute secrecy. He will not be shocked by sins, and, as a sinner, goes to Confession himself.

No sense of sin. Even the saints practised Confession regularly. A properly formed and examined conscience will give a true understanding of our sins (c.f. 1 Jn 1:8).

Unfamiliar. The basic formula is very simple and is good to learn. The priest will also guide those out of practice.

A simple form of Confession

CONFESSION

Make the Sign of the Cross and say: "**Bless me Father, for I have sinned. It is** (*state how long*) **since my last Confession. These are my sins** (*state the kinds of sins and the number of times*). **For these and all my sins, I am very sorry**".

PRIESTLY ADVICE AND PENANCE

The priest gives advice and a penance for after Confession.

ACT OF CONTRITION

"**O my God because you are so good I am very sorry that I have sinned against you. With the help of your grace I shall not sin again.**"

ABSOLUTION

The priest will then give absolution, by which sins are forgiven.

After Confession I should thank God and fulfil the penance the priest has given me. If I have accidentally forgotten to confess a mortal sin, I can be sure that the sin has been forgiven, but I must include it in my next Confession.

AN EXAMPLE 'EXAMINATION OF CONSCIENCE' – A SYSTEMATIC REVIEW OF ONE'S MORAL LIFE.

This example is based on the Ten Commandments (page 73)

1 Have I neglected to pray? Have I made any created things more important than God in my life? Have I engaged in superstitious practices such as astrology, fortune-telling, charms, spells, magic or the occult?

2 Have I given in to distractions in prayer? Have I abused or shown disrespect for holy places, objects or persons? Have I blasphemed by using holy names, such as swearwords? Have I broken a solemn oath or vow?

3 Have I missed Mass on Sunday or on a holy day of obligation without a serious reason? Have I engaged in activities on Sundays or holy days which have hindered the worship of God, works of charity or proper recreation?

4 Have I refused respect or care for my parents or religious superiors? Have I disobeyed lawful authority? Have I disobeyed my parents? Have I neglected my parents? Have I treated my children badly?

5 Have I murdered or co-operated in murder? Have I assisted suicide (euthanasia)? Have I committed or co-operated in abortion or IVF? Have I neglected the poor? Have I quarreled, fought, hated or been angry?

6 Have I committed adultery? Have I committed fornication? Have I engaged in masturbation or homosexual acts? Have I used artificial contraception? Have I lived with someone outside of Marriage?

7 Have I stolen anything, including goods, information, money or software? Have I failed to pay my taxes and debts to others? Have I paid unjust wages or misled my employer? Have I failed to return borrowed property?

8 Have I lied about another under oath? Have I lied about or exaggerated the fault of another? Have I lied in any other way? Have I damaged the good name of another? Have I made rash judgments about another?

9 Have I desired someone else's spouse? Have I looked at or thought of others as sexual objects? Have I engaged in impure fantasies? Have I used pornographic material of any kind? Have I engaged in impure jokes?

10 Have I been jealous of another's possessions, talents or looks? Have I disliked others because of their achievements? Have I measured my success by the failures of others? Have I failed to thank God for his gifts to me?

The right hand panel of *The Wilton Dyptich*

This pre-Reformation image illustrates the strength of traditional Catholic devotion to Our Lady and the saints in England. The Orb above the St George cross has a miniature image of England.

Catholic Devotions

A devotion is a customary popular prayer, often linked to other holy actions, objects or places.

Devotions are good because they help form habits of prayer, they are shared with others and they help to sanctify people, places and things. Their diversity meets different needs and expresses some of the richness of the kingdom of heaven.

Devotions of the Liturgical Year

ADVENT AND CHRISTMAS

Advent is the four-week period of preparation for the coming of Jesus Christ, celebrated at **Christmas**. The most popular devotion during Advent is the **advent wreath** containing four candles that are lit one after the other on the Sundays leading up to Christmas. At Christmas it is customary to erect a **crib**. This is made up of model figures of the baby Jesus, Mary, Joseph and others grouped according to the scene at Bethlehem where Jesus was born.

LENT AND EASTER

Lent is the period of forty days in which we prepare, by prayer, fasting and penance, for the celebration of the death and Resurrection of Jesus Christ at Easter. The most popular devotion during Lent is the **Stations of the Cross**, in which we walk and pray at fourteen stations that retrace the Passion of Jesus Christ from his condemnation to his entombment.

Ordinary Time covers the rest of the year. It includes, however, some major solemnities and feasts. On **Corpus Christi** it is customary to carry the Blessed Sacrament in solemn procession. We especially honour the Blessed Virgin Mary during May and October, and on the **Assumption** we honour her by a procession and by crowning her statue. Many Catholics prepare for the major feasts by a **novena**, a series of prayers over the preceding nine days.

Devotions to the Holy Eucharist

Eucharistic adoration is the worship of Jesus Christ, present under the appearance of bread. It is customary to expose the Eucharistic host in a monstrance for a set period of time outside Mass. Most parishes set aside at least an hour a week for Eucharistic adoration.

Benediction is the rite of blessing with the Eucharistic host given by a priest or deacon. It is customary to sing (for example, *Tantum Ergo*) and incense the host during Benediction.

Devotions to the Blessed Virgin Mary

The Rosary is series of prayers which brings to mind 20 of the main events in the life of Jesus and Mary. For each of the 20 mysteries (5 joyful, 5 luminous, 5 sorrowful and 5 glorious) we pray a 'decade', which is: one *Our Father*, ten *Hail Mary*'s and one *Glory Be*, following these prayers on a set of beads.

The many other Marian devotions include the **Angelus**, which is prayed at 6am, noon and 6pm, the **Litany of Loreto**, wearing the **Brown Scapular** and the **Miraculous Medal**.

Devotions to the saints and the dead

Patron saints accompany, help and intercede for us. We choose saints as our own patrons, especially at Baptism and Confirmation. Countries, occupations and activities also have distinctive patrons.

Praying for the dead in purgatory is a spiritual work of mercy. A common prayer for them is, *"Eternal rest grant unto them, O Lord, and let perpetual light shine upon them, may they rest in peace"*. It is also good to visit graves and pray for our deceased.

Shrines, pilgrimages and visits

A shrine is a church or other place of special devotion which, with the approval of the local bishop, is frequented by the faithful as pilgrims. Some popular examples are the shrines at Fatima, Lourdes and Walsingham. **A pilgrimage** is a journey to a shrine for the purpose of prayer and special intentions. Examples of **visits** are going to a church to pray before Christ in the tabernacle, or lighting a candle and praying.

Recommended devotions for the home

It is strongly recommended that every Catholic family pray the Rosary together regularly. It is also good to pray before and after meals and at the beginning and end of the day.

It is also spiritually beneficial for every home to have a crucifix and some holy image of Mary or the saints. Some homes have a little shrine where a candle can be lit and prayers said. A Bible in a prominent position is another good practice. A holy water font by the door enables those passing by to bless themselves with the Sign of the Cross.

Catechism of the Catholic Church

First Presented to the Faithful of the World
by Pope John Paul II, 11 October 1992

"A full, complete exposition of Catholic doctrine, enabling everyone to know what the Church professes, celebrates, lives and prays in her daily life."

Laetarum magnopere, 15 August 1997

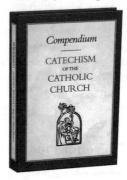

Compendium of the Catechism

Promulgated by Pope Benedict XVI
28 June 2005

"A faithful and sure synthesis of the Catechism of the Catholic Church."

Further Reading

Pope John Paul II declared the *Catechism of the Catholic Church* (1992) to be the sure and authentic reference text for all local catechisms. This compilation of further reading gives cross-references to the *Catechism* and to the *Compendium* (2005), the official synthesis of the *Catechism*.

SECTION		CATECHISM PARAGRAPHS	COMPENDIUM QUESTIONS
1	The Meaning of Life	27-49	1-5
2	Creation and Fall	279-421	51-78
3	Salvation History	50-64	6-8; 102
4	The Incarnation	422-486	79-104
5	The Life of Christ	512-570	105-111
6	The Paschal Mystery	571-667	112-132
7	The Trinity	199-267; 687-747	33-50; 136-146
8	The Church	748-962	147-195
9	Scripture and Tradition	74-141	6-24
10	Mary and the Four Last Things	964-975; 988-1060	94-100, 133-135, 196-199; 202-216

SECTION	CATECHISM PARAGRAPHS	COMPENDIUM QUESTIONS
11 Liturgy and Sacraments	1066-1211	218-250
12 Baptism and Confirmation	1213-1284; 1285-1321	251-270
13 The Eucharist	1322-1419	271-294
14 Confession and Anointing	1420-1532	295-320
15 Marriage and Holy Orders	1533-1666	321-350
16 Moral Action	407-409; 1264; 1730-1748; 1749-1761; 1776-1802; 1846-1876	363-376; 391-400
17 Natural Law and the Ten Commandments	1949-1964; 2052-2557	415-421; 434-533
18 Grace and the Beatitudes	1716-1729; 1812-1835; 1987-2029	358-362; 384-390; 422-428
19 Virtues and Vices	1803-1829; 1833-1844	377-383
20 Christian Life in the World	1877-1948; 2012-2016; 2041-2043; 2201-2246; 2270-2283; 2351-2400	401-414; 428-433
21 The Life of Prayer	2558-2758	534-556; 567-577
22 The Lord's Prayer	2759-2865	578-598
23 Praying the Mass	1345-1355	271-294
24 The Practice of Confession	1422-1498; 2052-2557	296-312; 434-533
25 Catholic Devotions	2650-2696	351-353; 557-566

Subject Index

This lists the key pages for each topic rather than all references. More detailed explanations are found in the *Catechism of the Catholic Church* and *Compendium*.

Abortion, 85
Abraham, 16
Absolution, 60, 100
AD and BC, 23
Adam, 12
Adoration, 87
Adoration (Eucharistic), 104
Adultery, 73
Advent, 48, 103
Almsgiving, 48
Altar, 94
Angels, 13
Anger, 81
Annunciation, 19
Anointing of the sick, 49, 61
Apostles, 36, 65
Apostolic succession, 35, 65
Arianism, 21
Aristotle, 7
Ascension, 29
Assumption, 44
Astrology, 101
Atonement, 27
Avarice, 81
Baptism, 49, 51
Beatitudes, 76
Bible, 39, 41
Big Bang, 11
Bishops, 65
Blasphemy, 101
Blessed Sacrament, 95, 104
Body and soul, 11

Call to Holy Orders, 65
Cardinal virtues, 79
Catechism, 107
Catechumen, 52
Catholic (meaning of word), 35
Celibacy and Holy Orders, 65
Charity, 79
Chastity, 81
Chrism, 53
Christ, 19, 23, 27
Christian life, 83, 84
Christmas, 20, 48
Church, 35
Civil law, 71
Civil partnerships, 85
Cloning, 85
Cohabitation, 85
Commandments, 72, 73
Common good, 84
Communion, 55, 96
Communion of saints, 37
Concupiscence, 68
Confession, 59, 99
Confirmation, 49, 52
Conscience, 68, 101
Consecration (Mass), 97
Contraception, 85
Contrition, 60; act of, 100
Corpus Christi, 104
Covenant, 15
Creation, 11
Creed (Apostles'), 37

Creed (Nicene), 21
Cross, 27
Culture of death, 85
Damnation, 45
David, King, 17
Death, 44, 61
Decalogue, 73
Demons, 13
Determinism, 76
Devil, 13, 69
Devotions, 103
Deacons, 65
Diligence, 81
Dioceses, 65
Divorce, 63, 64, 85
Docetism, 21
Easter, 48, 103
Ecumenism, 37
Elijah, 17
Embryo, 85
End of time, 45
Envy, 81
Epiclesis, 97
Episcopate, 64
Eternal life, 44
Eucharist, 49, 55, 95
Eucharistic devotions, 104
Euthanasia, 85
Evangelisation, 84
Eve, 11
Evil choices, 8, 67
Evolution, 11
Examination of conscience, 101
Ezekiel, 17
Faith, 25, 79
Fall, 12
Family (basis of society), 73, 85
Fasting, 48, 84
Father, 73
Father (Trinity), 31
First cause (God), 7

Flesh (in evil sense), 69
Forgiveness, 35, 49, 75, 93
Fornication, 101
Fortitude, 79
Fraternal charity, 81
Freedom (moral action), 67
Friendship, 77
Friendship (with God), 9, 25, 33
Generosity, 81
Gifts of the Holy Spirit, 53
Gluttony, 81
God (natural knowledge of), 7
God revealed (Trinity), 31
Good choices, 8, 67
Gospels, 25, 38
Grace, 72, 75
Grave matter, 68
Guilt, 28
Habits, 79
Hail Mary, 21, 44
Happiness, 9, 75, 76, 87
Hate, 101
Healing, 24, 49, 59, 61
Heaven, 37, 45, 76, 92
Hell, 45
Holiness, 75, 76
Holy Communion, 57
Holy days of obligation, 82
Holy Orders, 49, 64
Holy Spirit, 32, 33, 53
Home (devotions), 105
Homily, 97
Homosexuality, 85
Hope, 79
Human beings, 8
Humility, 81
Immaculate Conception, 43
Immortality (soul), 8
Impurity, 73
In vitro fertilisation (IVF), 85
Incarnation, 19

Indulgences, 60
Infallibility, 40, 65
Inspiration (Scripture), 39
Intercession, 87, 97
Isaiah, 17
Israel, 16
Israel (new), 24
Jeremiah, 17
Jesus Christ, 19, 23, 27
John the Baptist, 17, 56
Judgment, 44
Justice, 79
Killing, 73
Kingdom of God, 23, 24
Knowledge, 68, 83, 88
Laity (lay faithful), 37, 47, 83, 84
Last Judgment, 45
Last Supper, 27, 56
Law, 36, 71, 72, 85
Laying on of hands, 65
Lent, 48, 103
Liberality, 81
Lie, 73, 101
Life, 7
Life of grace, 75
Liturgy, 47
Liturgy of the Word, 97
Lord's Prayer, 91
Love (charity), 79
Love of God, 24, 77, 88, 92
Love of neighbour, 24, 77
Lust, 81
Magic, 101
Magisterium, 40
Man (human beings), 8
Marriage, 49, 63, 85
Mary, the mother of Jesus, 43
Mass, 56, 95, 97
Matrimony (Marriage), 63
Meaning of Life, 7
Meekness, 77, 81

Mercy, 77, 82
Messiah, 15, 17
Modernism, 76
Moral action, 67
Mortal sin, 68
Moses, 16, 72
Mourning, 77
Natural law, 71, 84
Nestorianism, 21
New Testament, 25, 38, 39
Noah, 15
Novena, 104
Occult, 101
Old Testament, 38, 39
Orders, 49, 64
Ordinary Time, 104
Original Sin, 13, 51
Our Father, 91
Parables, 24
Parents, 11, 71, 73
Parish, 65
Paschal mystery, 27
Passion of Jesus Christ, 27
Passover, 56
Peacemakers, 77
Pelagianism, 76
Penance, 59, 100
Pentateuch, 38
Pentecost, 53
Perfection (nature and grace), 76
Persecution, 77
Persons (divine), 31
Persons (human), 11
Peter, 36, 40
Piety (devotions), 103
Pilgrimage, 105
Polygamy, 63
Pope, 36, 37, 40
Poverty, 77
Prayer, 87, 91
Praying for the dead, 105

Precepts of the Church, 82
Pride, 68, 81
Priests, presbyterate, 64, 85
Property, 73
Prophets, 17
Providence, 41
Prudence, 79
Psalms, 47
Punishment, 28, 45, 60
Purgatory, 37, 45
Purity of heart, 77
Reason, human, 8
Reconciliation, 59, 99
Redemption, 27, 55
Reparation, 60
Resurrection (Christ), 23, 29
Resurrection (end of time), 45
Revelation, 31, 39
Rites, 47
Rosary, 104
Sacraments, 48, 49
Sacrifice, 55
Saints, 37, 105
Salvation (atonement), 27
Salvation (sharing in God's life), 9
Salvation history, 15
Sanctifying grace, 75
Sanctus, 97
Satan (devil), 13, 69
Science and creation, 11
Scientists and God, 8
Scripture, 38, 39
Seal (Confirmation), 52
Second Coming, 29, 45
Self-control, 81

Seminary, 65
Sermon on the Mount, 24
Serpent (devil), 13
Seven deadly sins, 80
Sexual acts, 73
Shrine, 105
Sign of the Cross, 105
Sin, 67
Sloth, 81
Social teaching, 84
Society, 84
Solomon, 17
Soul, 8, 11
Stations of the Cross, 103
Suicide, 85
Sunday, 48, 82
Supernatural, 75
Tabernacle, 57
Temperance, 79, 81
Temple (Solomon), 17
Temptation, 69, 93
Thanksgiving, 87
Theft, 71
Theological virtues, 79
Tradition, 39
Transubstantiation, 57
Trinity, 31
Venial sin, 68
Vice, 80
Virtue, 79
Visits, 105
Vocation, 85
Works of mercy, 82
World (two senses), 69
Worship, 47